BETWEEN THE WARS

1919 – 1938

A CHRONICLE OF PEACETIME

A HISTORY IN PHOTOGRAPHS OF LIFE AND EVENTS, BIG AND LITTLE, IN BRITAIN AND THE WORLD SINCE THE WAR

PRC

INTRODUCTION

SO far the history books, and only the most up-to-date ones at that, all end at 1919. What happened after that is The Present. But the end of the war is twenty years ago now, and a lot more happens in twenty years these days than used to happen in forty years before the war.

In that short time there have been wars and threats of war ; we have had two new kings and five Prime Ministers ; the airplane has grown up and radio's little sister television is putting her hair up ; there has been a general strike and there have been the Bright Young People.

The speed of the succession of big events seems to put our time sense out a little. Was it only 1933 that Hitler became Chancellor? Was it as long ago as 1934 that Prince George married Princess Marina ? Was it as long ago as 1922 that we played put-and-take, as long ago as 1923 that Waterloo Bridge began to crack ?

When the professors write the history of the post-war years they will leave out "Oxford Bags" (1924), and the beginning of one-way traffic (1926). These pictures give you history, serious and not-so-serious ; the things that amused (and irritated) us, as well as the doings of nations and great men. They form an album of the events of your lifetime.

1919 THE YEAR OF VICTORY

That New Year's Eve which sang (and hiccupped) a welcome to the first year of peace began a long procession of almost hysterically gay crowds which took possession of London on every possible excuse. Life was not yet back to normal (it never has got back) : food was only beginning to be de-restricted—meat, sugar and butter coupons were not abolished until August ; five million men were taking time to demobilise, and were not finding jobs easily (1919 was the peak year for "ex-officers," not all genuine) ; and money was short. Any to spare, your country needed. The Victory (or "Peace and Joy") loan brought in forty million pounds in three days, and the smallest amount that could be invested was £5. The total was £700,000,000.

THIS was the spirit of England

Eros, always the centre of Britain's demonstrations of delight, was where you bought your flags and patriotic lapel pins. Relief and Victory were the emotions of the moment. Mr. Lloyd George's "Reconstruction" could wait, plenty of time for that. It was certainly our business to make Britain a land fit for heroes to live in; but first London must be a city fit for heroes to enjoy.

THAT

was the spirit in Germany: defeat, hunger, despair, strikes, revolution.

1919

Revolution—the destroyed Kaiser's palace in Berlin.

— MEANWHILE

"Hang the Kaiser" was the cry in England. The newspapers discussed who would be his judges when he was brought from Holland to the Tower of London, and what they would do with him. You were unpatriotic in those days if you suggested that his life should be spared—unless of course you took the line that hanging was too good for him ; there was the rival cry of "send the Kaiser to St. Helena."

When he fled to Holland a "Daily Express" reporter who had seen him before the war, said that during the four years his hair had gone completely white. There he remained, and application for his surrender after some months was refused.

So Germany had no Big Man any more . . .

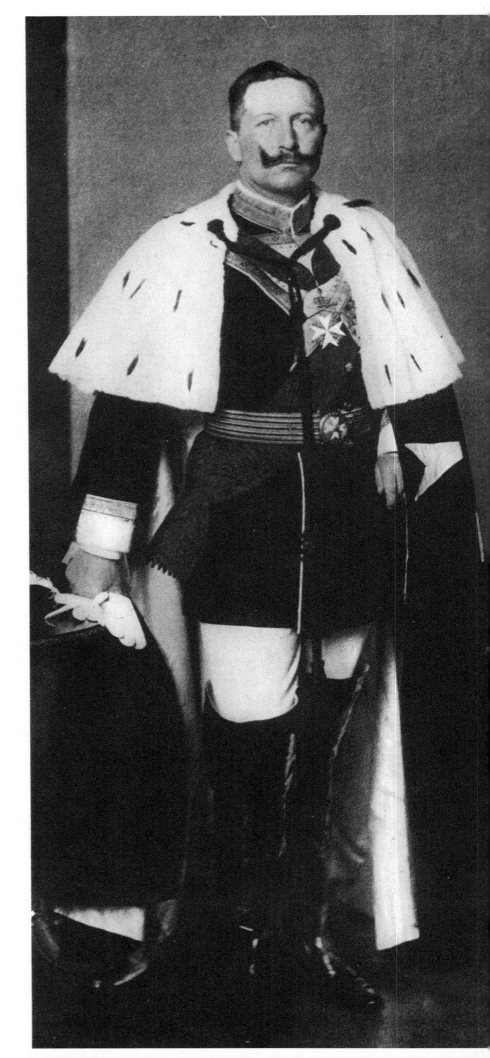

THE
FOUR BIG MEN

—of the moment were: the Prime Minister, Mr. Lloyd George; the Italian Prime Minister, Signor Orlando; France's Premier, M. Clemenceau; and Woodrow Wilson, President of the United States of America. They were the big figures at the Peace Conference held in Paris.

AND THE MAN
OF THE YEAR

was David Lloyd George, at the height of his power, the Man who Won the War. He was at the head of the Conservative-Liberal-Labour Coalition Government, returned at the General Election in December, 1918, with an overwhelming majority of more than 300 in the House of Commons; though the majority in the total of votes was strangely less marked—5,000,000 for the Government, 4,600,000 against.

7

1919

PEACE
was signed

in the Hall of Mirrors at Versailles, in June. Underlining the irony of the downfall of greatness is an inscription above the centre mirror which can be seen in Sir William Orpen's picture (from which this is taken). It says "Le Roy gouverne pour lui-même"—"The King governs on his own." The King referred to was guillotined a hundred and fifty years ago.

In the picture Germany's Dr. Johannes Bell is signing the Treaty which has given us so much trouble ever since. On Lloyd George's right are "Tiger Clemenceau and President Wilson. On his left Bonar Law and Arthur J. Balfour. Leaning over behind Lloyd George and Clemenceau is Sir Maurice Hankey, who is now secretary to the Cabinet.

PEACE
was
celebrated

in England with school holidays and dancing in the streets. The peace was properly organised (the Armistice of six months before had taken us unawares), and Peace Teas were gorged all over the country. The little girl in the gutter stood to attention for the camera man.

8

THE PEACE PROCESSION

in July was the Victory March through London in which the troops of 14 victorious nations (including Chinese and Portuguese) marched through London. Roses were thrown in the path of Sir Douglas (as he then was) Haig and of Marchal Foch. The cenotaph at that time was of plaster, designed by Sir Edwin Lutyens.

1919

LIFE BEGAN AGAIN . . . .

Feverishly. The Derby was run at Epsom again (a "false" Derby had been held at Newmarket during the war years). Here is Lord Glanely leading in his horse, Grand Parade, winner of the 1919 race, Fred Templeman up.

(Policemen had longer moustaches in those days, you notice).

But Slowly—

we were no longer fighting, but many of us were still soldiers—male *and* female. (Brighton beach was just as hard as it had been before the war).

THAT WAS A HOT SUMMER

—very hot, 1919. The grass was burnt yellow, and the cricket ball dropped like an iron cannon ball on the cracked earth. Victory weather, just right for a summer of Peace Parades and celebrations. And just right for those who had to sleep out: the returning warrior found London short of houses.

 PICCADILLY
was not a roundabout

In those days there was still room to move at a walking pace across Piccadilly Circus. Notice the "Old Bill" type bus, on what is now the wrong side of the street; as many men in uniform as not; "As You Were," on at the London Pavilion; the ageless violet seller installed on the steps of Eros.

THE SOLDIERS HAD COME BACK

—and the well-known blue uniform was seen about the streets. The wounded are cheerful because they are alive . . . During the war the Empire's death-roll was 900,000. More than two million were wounded. And only last January a man died as the result of a bullet wound received in 1918.

GERMAN FLEET SUNK!

The biggest news story of 1919 was the scuttling of the German grand fleet at Scapa Flow, eight months after its surrender. Of 74 warships interned, 48 sank within an hour when the German sailors opened the sea-cocks at the order of Admiral von Reuter. He said that he was obeying the Kaiser's orders, given him before the war, that no German battleship should be allowed to fall into enemy hands, and denied that he had broken the Armistice since he had had no notice of its extension beyond June 21, the day of expiry.

AT SCAPA FLOW

The German sailors risked their lives in carrying out their Admiral's orders. At noon on the 21st, the German ensign was run up, the battleships began to settle, and their crews crowded into boats or swam for it. Some of the British guardships, uncertain what was going on, opened fire, and there were over 100 casualties

NAMES THAT MADE NEWS were —

ALCOCK & BROWN
who flew the Atlantic
in this——

The next biggest story of 1919 was the first transatlantic flight. Captain Alcock and Lieutenant Whitten Brown left Newfoundland one tea-time, and landed at Clifden in Ireland 16 hours later. But they landed their Vickers-Vimy-Rolls bomber in a bog, so the first transatlantic flight was not without mishap; though they were themselves unhurt. London mobbed them, and they were both knighted. Only a year later Sir John Alcock was killed in an air crash in France.

On the way over they looped the loop, came through fog and ice nearly all the way, and set the fashion for later flights — coffee, chocolate, sandwiches.

In the picture above Mr. Winston Churchill is presenting them (Alcock is on the left) with a cheque for £10,000, prize-money for their flight.

YOU SEE HOW THEY LANDED

LADY ASTOR,
first woman M.P.,
went to the House
dressed like this

She was elected member for Plymouth in a by-election. Her speech after the declaration of the poll began: "Although I cannot say that the best man has won . . ." This first woman M.P. took the oath in the House sponsored by Mr. Lloyd George and Mr. Balfour. "I wish to be regarded as a regular working member" she said, "not as a curiosity."

SUZANNE

—Suzanne Lenglen played tennis dressed like this, and won the championship at Wimbledon for the first time.

FACES IN THE PAPERS—

IVY WOOD

ARTHUR BEARD

BILLIE CARLTON

—was a little girl of thirteen who lived in Cheshire. She was strangled by a night watchman, Arthur Beard, who was afterwards sent to a criminal lunatic asylum. The case was one of the two "big crimes" of 1919, and was remarkable as the first in which a murder appeal came before the House of Lords.

—was a young actress who died from an overdose of cocaine which she took after the Victory Ball at the Albert Hall. This was the start of the great drug traffic round-up which went on for some years.

AND—

They had just opened the first bit of the Great West Road; it must have been ideal for practice for L drivers. (So must the car). In 1919 only 300 Morris cars were turned out.

1920—
PEACE

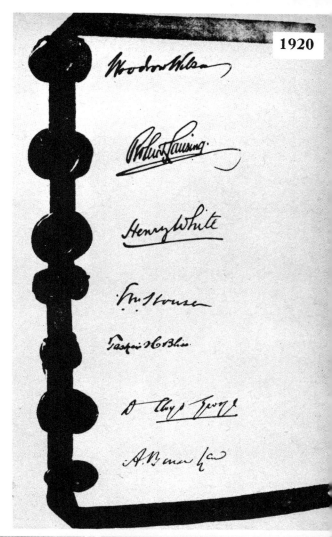

signed the year before at Versailles (here are facsimiles of some of the signatures on the Treaty), was finally ratified. President Wilson had insisted that the Covenant of the League of Nations must be part of the Peace Treaty, and thirty-one Allied States, together with thirteen neutral countries, had agreed to this. But America never ratified the Treaty, for when President Wilson returned from Europe, the vote in the Senate was 55 for, 39 against—and a clear two-thirds vote in favour was needed. Delegates from thirteen nations met at Geneva on January 10, 1920, the day the Treaty came into force.

This was the birth of the League of Nations. Here is its first meeting in London the following month. Mr. A. J. Balfour, then Lord President of the Council, is speaking. This was two years before he was made an earl. Sitting back from the table, two places to the left of Mr. Balfour, is Sir Eric Drummond, first Secretary General to the League of Nations.

AND THIS ROOM

in the Belgian hotel at Spa where the Kaiser had stayed before he abdicated, became a Press office for the British mission that had come to Spa for conferences on reparations. From March to November 1918, this place had been the seat of the German military headquarters in the west. The telephone used by the Kaiser stands on the table.

THE CENOTAPH

(meaning "empty tomb") was unveiled by King George V on Armistice Day, 1920. It took the place of the temporary memorial that had been erected for the Peace celebrations in July 1919; Sir Edward Lutyens, who designed it, deliberately omitted any religious symbol because the men it commemorated were of all creeds and none.

KING GEORGE the Fifth was fifty-five in 1920

We had emerged from the War with the monarchy stronger than ever. Four kings (of Bavaria, Prussia, Saxony and Wurtemberg) in Germany had been deposed ; the empires of Russia and Austria-Hungary had collapsed ; Greece, Turkey, and later, Spain, were to become republics.

Post war years in Britain brought strikes, unemployment, and in Ireland, civil war. But the King remained dissociated from politics and class-feeling, respected and liked by all. Here he is unveiling the Cenotaph in Whitehall on Armistice Day, 1920.

HOW THE UNKNOWN WARRIOR

The Unknown Warrior was first suggested by J. B. Wilson, then and now News Editor of the "Daily Express," in the issue of September 16, 1919. He wrote: "Shall an unnamed British hero be brought from a battlefield in France and buried beneath the Cenotaph in Whitehall?" The suggestion was adopted, but Westminster Abbey, not Whitehall, was chosen as the resting place.

Early in November, 1920, the bodies of six unknown men, killed in action, were brought to a hut at St. Pol, near Arras. The Unknown Warrior who was to receive an Empire's homage was chosen by an officer who, with closed eyes, rested his hand on one of the six coffins. This was the coffin that came to England.

Marshal Foch, greatest French soldier, salutes the Unknown Warrior at Boulogne as the coffin, brought from the hut at St. Pol, is conveyed to the British destroyer "Verdun."

Just before midday on November 10, H.M.S. "Verdun," with an escort of six destroyers, left Boulogne with the Unknown Warrior. The destroyer "Vendetta" met them half-way with its White Ensign astern at half-mast.

One hundred sandbags filled with earth from France, were sent over for the grave of the Unknown Warrior in Westminster Abbey. These porters are unloading the earth at Victoria Station.

King George V places a wreath on the Unknown Warrior's coffin, which rests on the gun carriage that is to take it from the Cenotaph to Westminster Abbey.

Field-Marshal Haig moves to help King George V. Queen Mary watched the ceremony from a balcony.

On the deck of H.M.S. "Verdun" four sailors stand guard over the coffin of the Unknown Warrior. The much-stained Union Jack draped over the coffin is covered with wreaths, with an anchor of flowers at the top.

The field-marshal's salute of nineteen guns was fired from Dover Castle as the Unknown Warrior arrived. Here is H.M.S. "Verdun" coming alongside Admiralty Pier in Dover Harbour.

Six officers, representing the Navy, Royal Marines, Army and Air Force, bear the coffin along the quay side from destroyer to the train. Troops lining the route are from the Dover garrison.

The Unknown Warrior is borne into Westminster Abbey, followed by King George V and the procession from the Cenotaph. Note the woman photographer with old fashioned camera.

Sentries from the four services, with arms reversed, stand at the corners of the coffin as it lies in state. One of the wreaths on the Union Jack is made of laurel from the ruined gardens of Ypres.

The grave of the Unknown Warrior is filled in. In the foreground are the empty sandbags, in the background were the flowers and wreaths that decked the coffin during the ceremony.

WOMEN
were news in 1920

The emancipation of the War had taught them that feminine talent could be just as useful in a public career as it was in the home. Oxford University acknowledged this on October 14, 1920, by conferring degrees for the first time upon fifty of their women graduates. But Cambridge held out against the feminine invasion. The first woman graduate to receive an Oxford degree was Miss Ivy Williams (picture on right). The new students were soon being labelled "undergraduettes" which brought a college protest : "The proper title for women students now is 'woman undergraduate,' and they do not desire to be known by any other name—slang or otherwise."

Mrs. Asquith (not yet the Countess of Oxford and Asquith), wife of the Liberal Opposition leader, began writing her memoirs during 1920 (see below). You see she is wearing "Russian boots." Do you remember the craze which was at its height five years later ?

The first "undergraduettes"

BIG TRIALS
were the
GREENWOOD CASE

Harold Greenwood, solicitor in the little Welsh village of Kidwelly, was arrested on June 16, 1920—just a year after his invalid wife had died—charged with murdering her by arsenic. Gossiping tongues had brought about the arrest and public prejudice was all against the solicitor.

Sir Marshall Hall, though a very sick man during the seven-day trial, defended Greenwood, who had to be given special police protection against crowds as he was driven to the assize court (right). By astute questioning of witnesses, by suggesting that the local doctor who attended Mrs. Greenwood had confused two bottles that looked alike—one holding bismuth, the other arsenic—Marshall Hall won his case. Greenwood, after four-and-a-half months in prison, awaited the jury's verdict for two and a half hours, then learned he was free. The crowds cheered him when he came out of the court.

and the crash of
FARROW'S BANK

Thomas Farrow, who had first made his name by exposing evils of usury, opened his bank in 1904 and had seventy-five branches in December, 1920, when they closed their doors. The bank had become insolvent, the annual trading loss being £1,000,000. As chairman and managing director, Farrow was arrested, charged with fraud and sentenced to four years penal servitude.

 SKIRTS
WERE LONGER

when Thomas Farrow was arrested for fraud. Women screamed hysterically outside the bank in Cheapside: "We want our money."

The men and women shown here were just few of the thousands of small depositors who lost their savings. Farrow's Bank had been founded expressly for poor people; accounts could be opened with £1.

THAT WAS 18 YEARS AGO

The Beggar's Opera

put on as a stop-gap in the hope that it would run for a month, actually went on at the Lyric Theatre, Hammersmith, for nearly two years. Old song tunes, and satirical dialogue made this show the most popular in Town. Frederick Ranalow played MacHeath and Vivian Roberts Polly Peachum in this 18th century British opera which was originally produced to lampoon politicians and other public characters of the day.

The Old "Cecil"

now gone, was on New Year's Day, 1920, the happiest and shabbiest hotel in England. Headquarters of the Air Ministry for three years it had, at last, been officially demobilised. Not until the last night of the year was the hotel reopened to guests.

Cowes . . .

was itself again when the Royal Yacht Squadron Regatta opened in glorious weather on August 3. King George V is aboard his yacht "Britannia" together with Queen Mary, Princess Mary and the Duke of York. The day before, this yacht had won the Big-Yacht race for a prize of one hundred guineas.

IRISH TROUBLES broke out again

A movement called "Sinn Fein" meaning "Ourselves Alone," had been organised during the War to separate Ireland from British rule. By 1920 opinion had become so bitter against the English that all through the year rebellion was breaking out in Ireland. Guerilla warfare, organised murder and arson was carried on in town and countryside. British troops were sent over and this picture shows the arrest of two men during a raid on the Ministry of Labour offices in Dublin.

The Funeral of the Lord Mayor of Cork

Alderman Terence McSwiney, Lord Mayor of Cork and an active Sinn Feiner, was arrested and sentenced to two years' imprisonment. In Brixton Gaol he declared he would starve himself to death to help his cause. He died on October 26 after a seventy-four day fast and his body was taken to Ireland. Here are mourners following his coffin through the streets to St. George's Roman Catholic Church, Southwark.

THE BLACK AND TANS

Next year, in 1921, Brigadier General F. P. Crozier was made Colonel Commandant of nearly six thousand soldiers, known from their uniform as the Black and Tans, who were to put a stop to the frequent shooting of policemen and attacks on police barracks by Irish gunmen. The Black and Tans adopted counter-terrorist methods ; at which Crozier protested and then resigned, forfeiting his pension. He accused high officials of a muddling and dangerous policy towards Ireland. The Black and Tans succeeded in creating an intense Irish hatred of British rule.

The Irish were praying in Downing Street

Public opinion forced the British cabinet to begin negotiations with the Irish Republican party. De Valera, then President of the Dail, was invited to London so that an Anglo-Irish treaty could be arranged. While the meetings were being held, Irish men and women knelt in Downing Street and prayed. The final treaty was signed on December 6, 1921, and the following month the Irish Free State came into being as a new Dominion.

VISITOR OF THE YEAR 1921

"I feel like Dick Whittington without a cat," said the man who, leaving London ten years before as an obscure music-hall artist, had returned in September 1921, as the world's greatest film comedian, to be greeted by fifteen thousand people at Waterloo station. Charles Chaplin, thirty-two years old, slight, trim waisted, dapper and diffident; the man who had made baggy trousers, big boots and a little bowler hat his trade-mark uniform.

Outside the "Ritz"

Crowds besiege "Charlie" as he arrives at his hotel in Piccadilly. Unable to move easily during the day, he did his sight-seeing by night, travelling to boyhood haunts in London slums, eating stewed jellied eels and forgetting (for a time) that he was now a millionaire.

ANOTHER VISITOR—

was Warwick Armstrong, great all-round cricketer who was criticised for his tactics as captain of the Australian team that came to England in the summer. Australia won the first three Test matches, so winning the Ashes. The fourth match was drawn and in the fifth, Armstrong took off his best bowlers, fielded in the deep and seemed—said the critics—indifferent to the result. When he retired from first-class cricket the following year, he had made more than 17,000 runs and taken more than 900 wickets.

☞ AND THAT YEAR

the Derby winner dropped dead. In the Derby, run in perfect weather and watched by record crowds, Mr. J. B. Joel's £100,000 "Humorist," with Steve Donoghue up, won by a neck from "Craig-an-Eran." Less than a month later, Charles Morton, the trainer, noticed blood trickling from beneath the stall door. When he threw back the door he cried unashamedly for "Humorist" was lying dead from hæmorrhage of the lungs.

CARPENTIER—

WAS KNOCKED-OUT BY—

DEMPSEY in the 4th Round

Ninety thousand people paid nearly £400,000 to see the great fight at Jersey City, U.S.A., on July 2 between Georges Carpentier, the Frenchman, and Jack Dempsey, the American, for the heavyweight championship of the world. It was anybody's fight up to three rounds; in the fourth, Carpentier was floored for a count of nine and immediately after, the knock-out came. He sprained his wrist and broke his right thumb in two places, while Dempsey was unmarked. Carpentier had come to the end of a grand boxing career.

THE R38 WAS BUILT

by the Admiralty and sold to the United States Navy; a million pounds hangar had been erected for her at Lakehurst, New Jersey. Here is the airship at Howden Aerodrome, just before setting off on her last flight. At five o'clock on the afternoon of August 24, after she had been out all night to complete trials, the R38 sent the message: "Landing at Howden 6.30 p.m."

Three-quarters of an hour later, as the great airship flew over Hull, her back began to break, there was an explosion and flames shot out along the outer casing. This picture shows all that was left of the R38 at the end of that day.

SHE FELL INTO THE SEA—

There were only five survivors when the R38, with forty-nine British and American officers and men on board, broke her back over Hull while making her final trial flight before going to America. Largest and fastest airship in the world at that time, weighing 83 tons with a speed of 60 m.p.h., depending for structural strength on sixty miles of piano wire used as stays and braces, the R38 cost £500,000. "I think it probable that several of the girders snapped when the airship turned while approaching the Humber," said Flight Lieutenant A. H. Wann, the airship's commander who was one of the survivors.

The Admiralty, chief builders and designers, published a report that the disaster was due to weakness in the framework. The Air Ministry, after investigation, reported that the disaster was due to structural weakness in the design.

Top picture shows the wreckage floating in the sea. The commander by heading her over the River Humber prevented R38 from falling on the city. In the lower picture of the wreckage, bodies can be seen caught in the twisted metal of the girders.

PRINCESS MARY ENGAGED

The betrothal of 24-year old Princess Mary to Viscount Lascelles, 39 year-old millionaire son of the Earl of Harewood, was officially announced from Buckingham Palace on Tuesday, November 22, 1921. (Her engagement ring was a single emerald ring, square cut). On the last day of the following February, the marriage was held at Westminster Abbey and the bridal bouquet was left by the royal Viscountess on the Cenotaph in Whitehall. The Abbey was thrown open to the public after the ceremony, and a mile-long queue was formed by people waiting to go inside.

BUCKINGHAM PALACE

It is with the greatest pleasure that the King and Queen announce the Betrothal of their beloved Daughter Princess Mary to Viscount Lascelles, D.S.O. eldest Son of the Earl of Harewood.

At a Council held at Buckingham Palace this evening His Majesty was pleased to declare his consent to the Marriage.

22nd. November, 1921.

Skirts were getting shorter now, they had moved from ankle to calf. Notice also the hat which Princess Mary is wearing as she walks with Viscount Lascelles through Harewood village. Below, Queen Mary driving in an open car (which looks strangely old-fashioned now) from Harewood to Leeds keeps tight hold of her hat. You can just see Princess Mary behind Lord Lascelles.

AND NEXT YEAR THEY WERE MARRIED

Crowds stood outside Buckingham Palace and cheered on the wedding day of King George V's only daughter to Lord Lascelles. The royal party came out on the balcony, which has figured in so many pictures in the last few years. From the right is Queen Mary, Queen Alexandra, the Queen Mother, widow of King Edward VII, who was now in her seventy-ninth year, Lord Lascelles, Princess Mary and King George V.

ALSO MARRIED

was the ex-Kaiser (whose first wife, by whom he had six sons and a daughter, had died in 1920) to Princess Hermine von Schonaich-Carolath. He had now settled down at Doorn to live the life of a country gentleman, spending his time, for exercise, chopping down trees. His Memoirs were published in England during 1922.

33

THE IRISH TROUBLES GREW

In Ireland, peace with England did not bring an end to fighting, for the Irish went on to fight among themselves. Michael Collins and Arthur Griffith had signed the treaty making the Irish Free State a Dominion ; De Valera, who had refused to sign because he wanted a Republic and not a Dominion, sided against his former colleagues. The Free State government and the Republicans could not reach an agreement and fighting broke out in Dublin. Buildings held by rebels were fired on by regular troops (right). The Four Courts (below) held by the rebels from April to July were destroyed with shrapnel and high-explosive shells (below, right).

34

WORSE AND WORSE

In England two Irishmen, Dunn and O'Sullivan, shot dead Sir Henry Wilson, brilliant soldier who had been elected M.P. for North Down. His outspokenness (he called the Home Authorities in the Great War "a Cabinet of all the indecisions"), and his speeches on the Irish question made him many enemies. The two gunmen had never been to Ireland, except for short holidays. They did not belong to the Republicans but they were against the treaty. O'Sullivan knew he would not escape arrest after his crime, for he had only one leg and could not get away quickly. Both men were hanged in August.

THIS SOLDIER

typifies the Ireland of 1922—a land of guerilla warfare with brother fighting against brother, father against son ; De Valera and Erskine Childers (an Englishman), at the head of the rebels, Collins, Griffith and Cosgrave at the head of the Treaty supporters. Dublin was a city of smoke and fire, from all parts of the country came tales of battles, ambushes, kidnappings and murders. This disturbance spread over the border into Ulster and for several weeks there was rioting in Belfast. Then in August, Arthur Griffith fell dead from heart-failure.

BUT PEACE WAS MADE

towards the end of the year by sterner military action against rebel terrorism. Many rebel leaders were captured and executed (including Erskine Childers), though De Valera still remained free. In December, Timothy Healy was sworn in as Governor General of the Irish Free State ; and the Duke of Abercorn was made Governor of Northern Ireland, a new state formed by six counties of Ulster that wished to remain attached to Great Britain.

Ten days after the death of Griffith, at the climax of the fighting, Michael Collins (above) Commander-in-Chief of the new Irish Free State, was murdered in an ambush in the south-west near Bandon, County Cork. His body was brought to Dublin to lie in state (right).

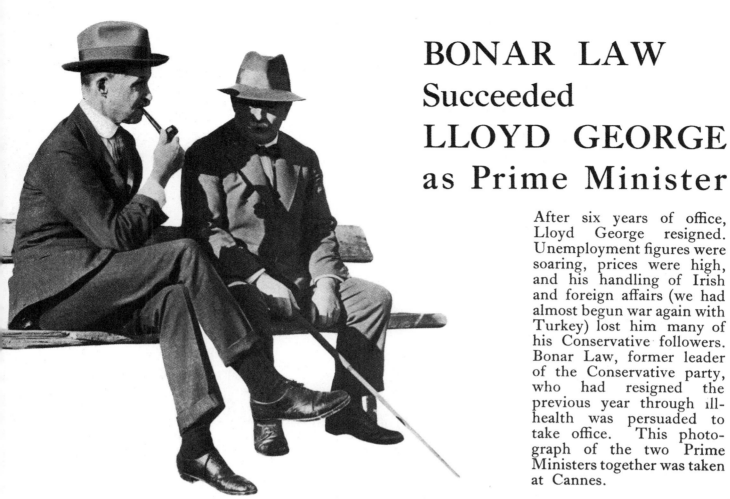

BONAR LAW
Succeeded
LLOYD GEORGE
as Prime Minister

After six years of office, Lloyd George resigned. Unemployment figures were soaring, prices were high, and his handling of Irish and foreign affairs (we had almost begun war again with Turkey) lost him many of his Conservative followers. Bonar Law, former leader of the Conservative party, who had resigned the previous year through ill-health was persuaded to take office. This photograph of the two Prime Ministers together was taken at Cannes.

And that year
LAWRENCE of Arabia
became Aircraftsman SHAW

T. E. Lawrence, the shy military genius who had practically single-handed aroused and organised the Arabs against the Turks, was called the "Uncrowned King of Arabia." In October, to escape publicity, he became a mechanic in the Royal Air Force under the name of Aircraftsman Shaw.

1922
BROADCASTING
BEGAN

from the famous London station 2LO on the top of Marconi House, Strand, in November, 1922. The British Broadcasting Company had been formed to send out short, regular "sponsored" programmes to the 8,000 people who had paid 15/- each for a "constructors licence." Listeners were often kept waiting while the piano was shifted; men in the studio were sometimes heard saying things that should never have been broadcast. But no listeners bothered much about these things. It was a miracle that anything was heard at all.

38

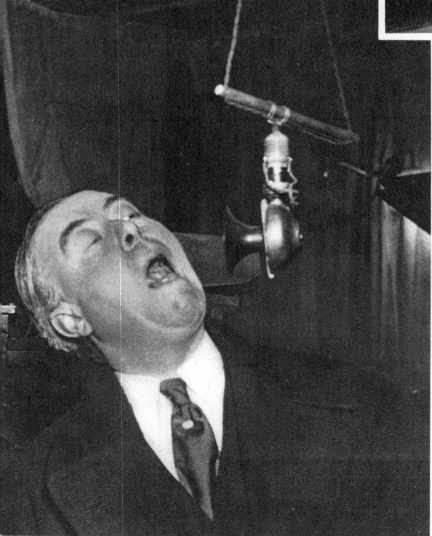

GEORGE ROBEY

was an early broadcaster. "The chief good it did was to help an old lady keep her maids. They were on the point of leaving but they listened in on her set and decided to stay." That was Robey's comment on early broadcasting.

ONE OF THE FIRST ANNOUNCERS—

was Arthur Burrows (above) who was in charge of the programme arrangements and later became known to thousands of listeners to the Children's Hour as "Uncle Arthur." One of the first commentators was Jack Dempsey, heavy-weight champion of the world, who described the Carpentier-Lewis fight in May, 1922. His round-by-round story from the ringside at Olympia was telephoned to the "Daily Express" broadcasting station at Slough, headquarters of the Radio Communication Company, and then sent out to the world.

. . . . and you listened on this sort of set, which was a very grand one. Sets had massive coils sliding in each other and an incredible amount of wire, which called for facetious remarks as to where the word "wireless" came in. Crystal sets, with "cats-whiskers" were cheap. They could be made for one shilling.

FAMOUS CRIMES OF 1922—

Remember the Thompson—Bywaters case?

Shortly after midnight on October 4, Thompson, walking home from Ilford station with his wife Edith, was stabbed several times in the back of the neck. Bywaters was the murderer, a twenty-years old youth who had been a lodger at the Thompson's home until the husband had found him making love to the wife and turned him out. Mrs. Thompson wrote passionate love letters to Bywaters, told him that she was trying to murder her husband with poison and ground glass. This was untrue, but Bywaters kept the letters and they were brought up at the trial. Both Mrs. Thompson and Bywaters were convicted, found guilty of wilful murder and sentenced to death. There was great public controversy . . . was Bywaters just a dupe? Did Mrs. Thompson say she was murdering her husband just to prevent Bywaters doing so? Would their appeal succeed? Public opinion received a shock. Together with her lover, Mrs. Thompson was hanged on January 9, 1923.

AND RONALD TRUE

handsome ex-airman who strangled and battered Gertrude Yates to death while on a visit to her flat. Before he came up for trial, an 18-year-old boy, Jacoby, had been sentenced to death for the murder of an elderly woman. True, though sentenced to death, was saved from the gallows by an order from the Home Secretary and he was sent to Broadmoor Asylum. Again there was much controversy; remembering Jacoby, people talked bitterly of one law for the rich, one for the poor.

ALLAWAY

a married, Bournemouth chauffeur, telegraphed to Irene Wilkins, who had advertised for a post as cook, telling her to come to Bournemouth. She travelled there from London and the next morning was found murdered on the outskirts of the town. Allaway was suspected, but the police had few clues. Then, after four months, a man was found who had seen the girl meet the chauffeur at Bournemouth station and drive away in a car. Allaway was brought to trial and found guilty. Mr. Justice Avory pronounced the death sentence and on August 19, eight months after his crime, Allaway was hanged.

SAME 👉
👇 MAN

BEVAN

Chairman of the City Equitable Fire Insurance Co., fled from London by airplane when the company failed, in February, with £4,000,000 losses. For five months he was a fugitive on the continent, until he was captured in Vienna, where he had grown a beard in an attempt at disguise. Back in London he was given a seven-year sentence for fraud.

AND BOTTOMLEY

orator, financier, journalist, was sent to prison for seven years in May, 1922, for fraudulent conversion of lottery funds. A man named Reuben Bigland had circulated thousands of pamphlets over the country attacking Bottomley as an arch-swindler. Bottomley charged him with criminal libel, dropped the case but carried on with a charge of blackmail. He lost and forty-eight hours later the Director of Public Prosecutions brought fraud charges against him. This was the end of Bottomley, a member of Parliament and a popular idol during the War because of his patriotic speeches.

That was the year of
PUT AND TAKE

William R. Pollard (right), a consulting engineer, had been watching some men throwing small brass tubes into a box. He picked up one of the tubes, filled it with wood, drove a nail through and spun it. He worked on the idea of this spinning top at home, made it hexagonal and put words on the sides: "Put One," "Take Two" and so on. Then he marketed it. At the beginning of 1922, Birmingham's brass foundries were turning out two million tops a week. Britain had fallen for the craze of "Put and Take." Later other words were printed—as you can see in the top photograph—to amuse the men of the country.

And the women? They were trying to look younger with make-up, lipstick, rouge and short hair. The short hair style adopted by women on war-work had become a fashion. Here is the bobbed hair style of the year.

—and of
BOBBED HAIR

42

He invented it

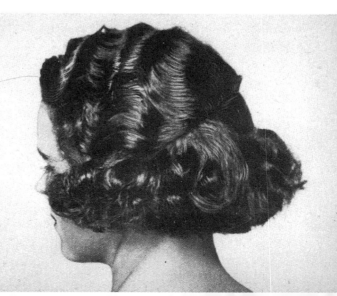

AND COUÉ . . . . . .

On page 22 you saw Miss Ivy Williams as the first woman graduate. Here she is now a "Double-first" or first woman barrister, lecturer in law at Oxford University. After the ceremony of being called to the Bar by the Masters of the Bench of the Inner Temple, port and madeira were handed round; but she drank water, saying: "To-night I have realised the dream of my life."

"Every day and in every way I am getting better and better"; this was the phrase of Emile Coué, short, stocky, grey-bearded French physician who founded a system of treating patients by auto-suggestion and came to London in 1922 to give demonstrations. His cult became a craze. He would say to his audience: "Clasp your hands, clasp hard, harder. Now say 'I want to loose them but I can't'," the claspers would strain to loosen their hands. "Think now" 'I can'" M. Coué would say. They did—and the hands would unclasp. For his last demonstration before he left England, he visited a hospital for shell-shock cases. His audience became hysterical and Coué had to leave. He treated the matter lightly, but one of the doctors said: "It put the work of the hospital back years."

THE "BLUE BOY"

was visited by one hundred thousand people early in 1922, when it hung in the National Gallery before being sent to Henry Huntingdon, the American who had paid £170,000 for it. Gainsborough's famous picture, formerly belonging to the Duke of Westminster, had been cleaned and these visitors saw it for the first time without its former coat of yellow varnish. Critics said the painting was now too blue, but the actual paint of the picture had not been worked on or touched at all during the cleaning. The sale of "Blue Boy" made people art-conscious in 1922. "We ought to find some way," they wrote to the newspapers "to prevent our great paintings being sent abroad."

THE GEDDES AXE

Government departments had got so used to spending freely during the War that they found it hard to cut down on their extravagance when it ended. A committee was set up under Sir Eric Geddes, notorious "big-business" spender during the war, to overhaul Civil Service expenditure. Sir Eric surprised everybody by making drastic cuts, so much so that the public began to talk about Geddes Axe. Sheffield made him one and Sir Henry Brittain, M.P. for Acton, gave it to him in his office.

LADY DIANA COOPER

Society beauty, daughter of the Duke of Rutland, wife of the present First Lord of the Admiralty, was seen in the £50,000 British natural-colour film "The Glorious Adventure" at the Royal Opera House, Covent Garden, in January, 1922. At the end of the film, she told reporters : "It was magnificent and far exceeding my expectations." "Daily Express" critic wrote : "Lady Diana is not yet a great actress. She has ability but it shows timidly. She is afraid to let herself go." Her next film was "The Virgin Queen" shown in 1923, in which she played the part of Queen Elizabeth. In that year, Lady Diana, prominent in amateur theatricals, was chosen for the part of the Madonna in "The Miracle" to be played in New York. Here she is as the Madonna, with Lily Elsie as an angel. The four lower pictures from left to right, show Lady Diana dressed as a nun in "The Miracle" ; wearing her costume as Queen Elizabeth ; dressed as Britannia for the Heart of Empire Ball, 1922 ; watching minor scenes in the filming of "The Virgin Queen."

ABROAD —

In Germany, the mark dropped in exchange value to 1,810 to the £; Its pre-war rate had been 20.43; 75 million billion paper marks were backed by only 722 million gold marks. Rathenau, brilliant Jew who had been made Minister of Reconstruction, intended to rid Germany of reparations and debts by inflating the currency. He planned to hold the mark at 300 to the £, but in June, he was assassinated by young fanatics. Without Rathenau there was no·control over the mark. Everybody in Germany with fixed salaries or small savings was ruined. In Britain children in the streets played "bricks" with wads of German banknotes.

And in EGYPT —

the tomb of King Tutankhamen, who had ruled Egypt three thousand years before, was discovered by Mr. Howard Carter and Lord Carnarvon in the Valley of the Kings at Luxor after a seventeen years search. A world-wide legend arose that a curse was inscribed on the tomb: "Death shall come on swift wings to him that toucheth the tomb of a Pharoah." But this was not the case, though the death of Lord Carnarvon the following year caused superstitious comment. Here is Mr. Howard Carter super-vising the packing of the treasures that had been found.

IN ITALY–

Mussolini, journalist, son of a blacksmith and strong Socialist during the War, was organising a Fascist movement among the enemies of Socialism. His followers were mostly "big business" men, army officers and the middle classes of central Italy who disliked the policy of State enterprise and demanded a return of private ownership. In October they seized public buildings in many towns and then marched on Rome. The King, knowing that the army was sympathetic, called Mussolini and asked him to form a ministry. In this picture Mussolini, in a lounge suit, leads the march through Rome.

AND IN AMERICA

Dorothy Gish, comedy actress, was playing the tragic part of a blind girl in the new D. W. Griffith's film "Orphans of the Storm," a tale of two little country girls in Paris at the time of the Revolution. Lilian Gish co-starred with her sister. This film had taken eight months to make at Long Island studios. Griffiths, with no written scenario, took 500,000 feet of film, cut it to 12,000 feet, wrote nearly all the sub-titles (films were silent remember), selected musical accompaniment and composed new tunes. When shown in London in March, the film lasted two and a half hours. Wrote the "Daily Express" critic : " 'Orphans of the Storm' is colossal. Women in the audience turned their heads away or closed their eyes. Men gripped the arms of their chairs a little more tightly."

DONOGHUE AGAIN!

In the paddock, just before the Derby was to be run, "Captain Cuttle," owned by Lord Woolavington, formerly "Jimmy" Buchanan, whisky king, was found to be lame. Steve Donoghue, after mounting him, got off and felt the colt's legs. The nail in a loose plate causing the lameness was taken out and the affected part dosed with cocaine. In miserable style "Captain Cuttle" cantered past the stands up to the starting post. But the lameness had gone when the crowds shouted "They're Off!" and "Captain Cuttle" finished easily, four lengths in front of Lord Astor's "Tamar"—giving Donoghue his fourth Derby and second successive win.

AND DO YOU REMEMBER–

the woman who tried to start a knickerbocker fashion in England? Jane Burr, small, dark-eyed American Jewess, arrived from New York in August, 1922, in a vivid green woollen jumper and tweed knickerbockers. But this stunt was only part of her campaign to improve woman's position in life. She advocated "progressive monogamy" —a changing of husbands at intervals of three years because "marriage as it now exists is an almost intolerable relationship. The average length of an 'undying affection' is three years." By the end of the year, Jane Burr had decided to abandon her knickerbocker costume and wear frocks. Her ideas had not gone down too well.

IN 1923 A MR. BALDWIN BECAME PREMIER

This country did not know him as they do now. For eight years he had been a quiet but popular Parliamentary back-bencher, until in 1917 at the age of fifty he became Finance Secretary to the Treasury. At the Carlton Club in 1922, he moved that the Conservatives fight the general election as an independent party with their own programme and their own leader. The party came into power. Stanley Baldwin was Chancellor of the Exchequer and in May, 1923, with the resignation of Bonar Law, he stepped up into place as Premier. Even then he had a favourite pipe. See it in his left hand?

☞ LORD CURZON

Foreign Secretary and leader of the Conservative Party in the House of Lords, had hoped, with his greater experience, to be chosen instead of Baldwin, as Britain's Prime Minister. But he took the disappointment well and consented to take the chair at the meeting which elected Baldwin to the leadership.

1923

AND THIS
NOW FAMOUS
FACE

belonged to the Minister of Health, Arthur Neville Chamberlain, then fifty-four years of age. For nearly half a century he had kept out of politics, had helped run the family business of making screw nails and extended his influence in Birmingham till in 1915 he had been made Lord Mayor of that city. Three years later he had surprised everybody and entered Parliament. Why? Because his wife, who came from an Irish sporting family, urged him to. Said Mrs. Chamberlain of her husband: "He would never have gone into politics but for me."

Here he is leaving Buckingham Palace with the Minister of Agriculture, Mr. E. F. Wood, now Lord Halifax; in the top picture, he is shaking hands with a chef, after opening Hornsey's Clean Food Exhibition.

POLITICALLY IMPORTANT—

Margaret Bondfield, Labour politician, first woman Cabinet Minister in Britain, and elected president of the Trades Union Congress in May, was a former shop assistant who worked untiringly to better the conditions of shop assistants. In the December elections she won her seat at Northampton with a majority of more than four thousand.

AND IN MUNICH

ex-corporal Hitler, former house painter, was sent to jail. In 1921, he had begun to appear in Munich beer gardens, preaching from table-tops against the German government, the Versailles Treaty, capitalists and Jews. He said to journalists : "If Germany could be given a Mussolini, the people would kneel down and worship him." Two years later, with General Ludendorff as his patron, he was leader of a National Socialist party which, on November 9, marched into Munich as first stage in a march on Berlin. The insurrection collapsed under fire from Bavarian police ; Ludendorff, in black coat and top-hat, marched on and bullets missed him. Hitler vanished, was captured two days later and charged with high treason. Here he is, "the man in the raincoat" standing next to Ludendorff, just before the trial.

AGAIN THE BALCONY . . .

The present King, was the first of King George V's sons to marry. As Duke of York he married a commoner, Lady Elizabeth Bowes-Lyon, youngest daughter of the Earl of Strathmore, on April 26, 1923. After the wedding, crowds gathered outside Buckingham Palace, looked up to the familiar balcony and cheered when Queen Alexandra, Queen Mary, the Duchess of York (soon to be known as "the smiling Duchess"), the Duke of York and King George V came out through the central French windows. King George V was already a grandfather, for Princess Mary, married the year before, had given birth to a son in February.

The Duchess started a vogue for lace. Her bridal gown, designed from an Italian painting, was of chiffon moire, its colour the ivory shade of old lace. The corsage, with severe lines, was embroidered in silver and pearl, and for her veil white tulle was chosen with a light wreath of orange blossom. In the train—lent by the Queen—there was more lace.

This was the wedding in the Abbey. Just above the bride can be seen, in dark uniform, the boyish-looking Prince George (now Duke of Kent) and beside him, Queen Mary and King George V. The Prince of Wales, as the Duke of Windsor was then, standing just behind the altar rail, moved his head as the photograph was taken. The Duke of Gloucester is behind him.

Facsimile of the marriage certificate is shown below.

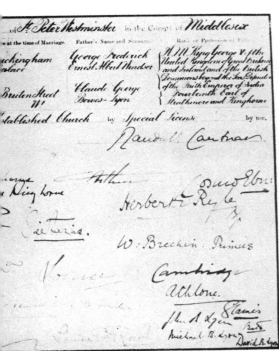

ANOTHER ROYAL WEDDING THAT YEAR

was on November 12, between Princess Maud, daughter of the Princess Royal, Duchess of Fife, to Lord Carnegie, son of the Earl of Southesk. This informal snapshot shows King George V, Queen Mary and the royal brothers after the ceremony.

THE PRINCE OF WALES WAS THEN 29

As the Empire's Ambassador he was becoming the best known man in the world. Since the War he had toured Canada and the United States, Australia, New Zealand and the West Indies, India, Burma and Japan. He had bought a ranch in Alberta during his Canadian visit and went off to see it in September, 1923. In April he had gone to Brussels with Earl Haig (right) to unveil the Anglo-Belgian Memorial.

BIG NEWS THAT YEAR

In a screaming gale, the 5,000 ton Cornish cargo boat "Trevessa" with water pouring through her broken plates and laden down with a soggy cargo of zinc concentrates, sank into the Indian Ocean at three o'clock on the morning of June 4, 1923. The forty-four men who had got away in two open boats—one under Captain Cecil Foster, the other under First Officer Charles Smith—were 1,600 miles from Australia, 1,750 miles from Mauritius. Ships that answered the S O S reported to London that there could be no hope of survivors. Britain forgot the "Trevessa." But twenty three days later, Foster's boat reached land at Rodiguez after sailing 1,700 miles. On June 29, Smith's boat reached Mauritius after sailing 2,100 miles in twenty-five days. The 1789 feat of "Bligh of the Bounty" had almost been equalled.

England welcomed them home the following January; Foster and Smith were called to Buckingham Palace to receive the congratulations of King George V. Said Captain Foster, later: "After all, we only did our share, each of us, in bringing the boats to safety."

Here is a survivor recounting his experiences to newspaper reporters.

This boat, so small that there was room only for the twenty men in her to sit up all the time, sailed 1,700 miles under Captain Foster. Two Indian firemen died from exposure during this voyage. In Smith's boat, nine men died. All the sailors were weak, having lived only on rations of one ship's biscuit and one-third of a tin of water each day.

ALSO NEWS

was the beginning of a long story ; in December, the centre piers of Waterloo Bridge subsided (almost eight inches in one spot), and a definite curve could be seen in the roadway. The London County Council called in bridge experts to inspect it. Waterloo Bridge, designed by John Rennie and opened in 1817, was regarded as the finest in London, one of the most beautiful in Europe, and a great deal of controversy followed the suggestion that a new bridge should be built. The battle of Waterloo Bridge really began the following year when increasing cracks convinced engineers that a new bridge was needed.

THE NEW REGENT STREET

was going up ; ferro-concrete buildings were replacing the dignified architecture of John Nash who had designed the street, named after the Prince Regent, later George IV, as part of a town-planning scheme. Eros points to the old Swan & Edgar building which was shortly to come down. This store had just escaped demolition in 1917, when a German Zeppelin dropped a 2-cwt. bomb in front of it, killing nine people, injuring seventeen. The picture below shows the famous Quadrant as it was in 1886.

57

THIS MAN

was becoming powerful in world affairs. Mustapha Kemal Bey (now Kemal Ataturk), professional soldier who successfully defended the Dardanelles against wartime British attacks, had smashed and driven the Greeks out of Turkey in 1922. Britain had backed Greece to win and this unexpected victory brought us almost to war with Mustapha Kemal. A rug-maker's son, despotic, hard-living, a gambler, soon to be Dictator of Turkey, he was determined to westernise his country. He planned to free women from the harem, bring in new educational systems, abolish the veil and the fez. His hair was grey, and his face, sallow from suffering from an internal complaint, brought him the nickname "Grey Wolf."

THIS WOMAN

died in her Paris home in the Boulevard Periere on March 26, 1923, an imperious dame of seventy eight with a wooden leg—Sarah Bernhardt. Greatest tragedienne of her times, she had prepared for death long before. Her rosewood coffin lined with white satin had been in her possession for thirty years and had gone with her on world tours. "I want flowers, more flowers," were her last words, and the world sent enough to fill five wagons which followed the bier along a route lined by more than six hundred thousand people.

That was the year of the Cup Final Stampede—

were you one of those who tried vainly to get in at Wembley?

Three hundred thousand people hoped to see the first Wembley Cup Final match between Bolton Wanderers and West Ham United ; two hundred thousand of them entered the Stadium which was designed to hold 125,000 only. Barriers were stormed, mobs climbed fences, the playing field was invaded and the game held up for three-quarters of an hour ; ambulance men attended to one thousand casualties. Nobody would accept responsibilty for the disorder. But the hero of the whole show was a police inspector on a snow-white, prancing horse, who started from the middle of the ground, slowly edged back the crowds and cleared a space. And the game ? Bolton Wanderers beat West Ham United by two goals to one.

ABROAD
TOKIO

and several other large cities in Japan were suddenly shaken into ruins which then caught fire. The sea swept in over the land, hills fell down on the suburbs, streets opened and traffic fell into great fissures. The earthquake of September 1 killed 400,000 people in Yokohama alone and injured as many more. Japan, disappointed with her War rewards and planning at that time to build an Empire, never made public the full loss.

THE RUHR

was entered by the French who insisted that the Germans were cheating them in delivery of coal from that region. Nearly 50,000 men, escorted by armoured cars and whippet tanks, marched in to occupy Germany's greatest industrial area. They expected war, but instead met with passive resistance. Every industrial leader and chief official had left; the organisation controlling coal output had been broken up.

CALLING VERY FEW CARS!

A firm of radio dealers in the E End of London found a new advertising stunt in 1923. They fitted a three-wheeled runabout with radio and sent it touring the streets, relaying concerts to the public. This "listen while you drive" effort, anticipated car-radio by more than five years.

CARPENTIER & "C.B."

Joe Beckett, heavy-weight champion of England had clamoured four years for a return fight with Carpentier, who had knocked him out in the first round in their 1919 contest. Fifteen thousand people gathered in Olympia on October 1st to watch Beckett prove that the 1919 first-round blow was a fluke. The bell sounded—and fifteen seconds later, Beckett slumped to the floor, knocked out once again by Carpentier's right. C. B. Cochran handed a Gold Cup over to the Frenchman after the fight.

FIRST LABOUR GOVERNMENT

At the end of 1923, Mr. Baldwin's government fell. Stanley Baldwin went to the country on a programme of Protection and Imperial preference —but without food taxes. He was defeated, and the next January, Ramsay MacDonald, leader of the Socialists, took office. For the first time in history, Britain had a Labour Government. The country wondered how the new Ministers would act. Would they fly in the face of time-honoured formalities? Tom Griffiths, Socialist Treasurer of the Household who had been a Welsh tinplate worker, told afterwards how King George V met his Labour Ministers:

"None of us felt in the least embarrassed with such a kindly host. We all made friends at once and he gave us lucid instructions about our duties, not without a touch of humour."

Above are the Socialists, Ramsay MacDonald, J. H. Thomas, Arthur Henderson and J. R. Clynes after leaving the Palace.

THE NOVELTY OF MR. THOMAS DRESSED UP

had no sooner worn off than Labour was out again. They had been in office only nine months. Like the previous government they had done little to reduce the high unemployment figures. MacDonald however, had initiated a revision of German reparations that was to lead to partial relief of Europe's financial troubles.

👉 MR. BALDWIN

by now a famous figure, pipe-smoking, solid, a countryman and an amiable politician who appeared to be a frank practical business man, found himself Prime Minister once more, with an absolute Conservative majority.

LABOUR FELL BECAUSE—

—THE ZINOVIEV LETTER BOMBSHELL BURST

On October 25, in the week before the general election, London newspapers published a letter purported to come from a Moscow Commissar, Zinoviev, which gave instructions to British Communists to prepare for revolution. Ramsay MacDonald had known of the letter for two weeks and had sent copies to the Foreign Office but not until newspapers had heard of the letter did the Foreign Office hurriedly publish official details together with the draft of a strong protest to the Soviet Government. Publication had been delayed, they said, until the authenticity of the letter had been proved. The British public, however, resentful of foreign interference in their home affairs, swung away from the Socialists and sent Conservatives back to power.

But even in England, as in other countries where the workers are politically developed, events themselves may more rapidly revolutionise the working masses than propaganda. For instance, a strike movement, repressions by the Government, etc

From your last report it is evident that agitation-propaganda work in the army is weak, in the navy a very little better. Your explanation that the quality of the members attracted justifies the quantity is right in principle, nevertheless, it would be desirable to have cells in all the units of the troops, particularly among those quartered in the large centres of the country, and also among factories working on munitions and at military store depots. We request that the most particular attention be paid to these latter.

"EVENT OF WAR."

In the event of danger of war, with the aid of the latter and in contact with the transport workers, it is possible to paralyse all the military preparations of the bourgeoisie and make a start in turning an imperialist war into a class war. Now more than ever we should be on our guard Attempts at intervention in China show that world imperialism is still full of vigour and is once more making endeavours to restore its shaken position and cause a new war, which as its final objective is to bring

ZINOVIEV

following publication of the letter, denied that he had written it and denounced it as a forgery. The Soviet Government demanded an apology for the charges of propaganda activity laid against them. But the Foreign Office repeated that they were quite satisfied the letter was genuine. Three years later Zinoviev was expelled from the Communist party, and in 1936 was shot in prison at Moscow.

HE WAS A "CHARACTER"

During his twenty-six years on the Bench, Mr. Justice Darling, who retired in 1923, and was given a peerage on New Year's Day 1924, became the most widely known of England's criminal judges. This short, slight man with the sharp-featured face and keen intellect, came to be looked on as a "character." He would be cold, austere, then suddenly playful and almost waggish. Very few of his cases were ever reported without the bracketed phrase—Laughter in Court.

These were among his witticisms : To a witness who said he went to the "Elephant" Inn to telephone, "A trunk call, I presume ?"

To a woman witness : "You have repeated the same thing so often that you make me think I am back in the House of Commons."

To a long-winded barrister who complained that the echo in court brought all his words back to him : "You have my sympathy."

"How long have you been a widower ?" he asked a doubtful witness who had said he had been wedded to the truth from infancy.

Lord Darling published a book of epigrams. Some of them are :

The chief difference between prisoners and other people is, perhaps, captivity.

It is a fault of cheap justice, as of gin, that it is purchased by many who were better without it.

We always suspect the honesty of those who are actuated by motives which would not influence ourselves.

If a man stays away from his wife for seven years, the law presumes the separation to have killed him ; yet, according to our daily experience, it might well prolong his life.

1924

WEMBLEY

1924

ARE YOU IN ANY OF THESE PICTURES ?

Two hundred thousand people, eleven Cabinet Ministers and nearly fifty members of British and foreign Royalty attended the opening by King George V, of the British Empire Exhibition at Wembley, April 23, 1924. "We hope" he said "that the success of the Exhibition may bring lasting benefit not to the Empire only, but to mankind in general." A few minutes later, a messenger boy handed him a large, white envelope—a telegram, announcing the opening, which had gone round the world in eighty seconds.

Later, King George and Queen Mary rode on the miniature railway and strolled, under sunshades, through the terraces, summing up the whole exhibition with the words : "The whole Empire in little !"

Wembley surpassed all previous exhibitions. You paid your one-and-sixpence and had fifteen miles of sightseeing in front of you. One million poundsworth of jewellery were on view; you could stare at the world's smallest watch or a 2½-ton silver nugget. You could wander through the showplaces of eighteen Dominions and colonies, the Palaces of Engineering, Industry and Art, or have a good laugh in the 40-acre Amusements Park. There were six concerts a day to listen to, one hundred thousand flowers to look at, replicas of the Taj Mahal, Tutankhamen's Tomb, or a West African mud village, to hold your interest. Even after several visits most people felt they hadn't seen a half of it.

MUCH CRITICISED

but not without a certain beauty, the £12,000,000 Exhibition finally closed down in October, the following year, after having been seen by 28,000,000 people. The total loss was £2,000,000, but all Dominions and Colonies reported : "It has been more than justified from our own particular point of view."

THAT YEAR THERE WERE FLOODS

in south and east England, owing to heavy winter rains. Tradesmen and postmen called at low-lying bungalows and houses in waders, boats and punts. The Thames at Teddington could take, at the most, $4\frac{1}{2}$ million gallons a day without flooding. The daily flow in January was sometimes a million gallons more than this.

SALVAGE 👉

at Scapa Flow (see Page 12) was begun by a Queenborough firm who undertook to raise 24 destroyers and two battle cruisers of the sunken German fleet. When the divers went down they found the ships covered in seaweed, with stalks twenty feet long and thick as a man's wrist. Chief Diver Mackenzie, who had been diving in all parts of the world for fifteen years, said: "I have never seen this kind of weed so large."

71

LENIN, founder of the New Russia, DIED

at fifty-three years of age on January 21, 1924, from brain disease brought on by overwork. He had changed his real name, Vladimir Ilyich Ul'yanov, when he was a young man, after he had been sent to Siberia for revolutionary activity. He came to London in 1903, and in lodgings near King's Cross worked on his future plans, spending hours of study each day in the British Museum. At these lodgings he first met a new comrade, Trotsky, just escaped from Siberia. Russia was not safe for Lenin, leader of international socialism, until 1917. Then came the Revolution. In Moscow, as shown in this photograph, Lenin, slightly squat with large domed head, Trotsky and their comrade Kameneff (leaning against the platform) expounded their doctrines to the Russian workers. At death, Lenin became the Red Saint, his body embalmed beneath glass in a magnificent granite tomb became the Soviet shrine and is visited now by two thousand people each day.

BY 1925 MR. BALDWIN'S PIPE WAS SO FAMOUS

THAT any facts about it made news. He confessed, in January, that he never paid more than three shillings for a pipe; revealed, in June, that he smoked an ounce of tobacco a day. When given the freedom of his native town, Bewdley, Worcs., in August, he was also given the pipes shown here. (He now had 7,000). In the picture below, he is watching Sir Austen Chamberlain sign the Locarno Treaty in December, which was to bring Germany into the League of Nations.

74

EROS CAME DOWN
early in 1925 (pushing the face of one of the workmen during the process) to be out of the way of contractors working on the reconstruction of Piccadilly Tube Station, which was to be built in oval form under the circus. It was six years before Eros came back.

☜ JACK HOBBS BEAT RECORD SET BY W. G. GRACE

Playing against Somerset at Taunton on August 17, 1925, Jack Hobbs, after making ninety-nine runs, raised his bat, hit the ball and ran for a single. The man at the scoreboard calmly put up the hundred, then the game stopped for five minutes while ten thousand onlookers jumped, gasped, cheered, clapped and waved their hats in the air. This forty-two year old Surrey batsman had equalled W. G. Grace's record of 126 centuries in first-class cricket. To his wife he sent the telegram : "Got it at last" and the following day he made another century and broke the record.

THIS MAN ☞ INVENTED SUMMER TIME

William Willett, London builder who died in 1915, was ridiculed when he first suggested saving daylight by putting clocks forward an hour during summer. A year after his death the scheme was adopted as a wartime economy measure, and in 1925 an Act of Parliament made it permanent.

TRAIN NUMBER ONE —100 YEARS AFTER

With black fumes belching from its tall smoke stack, George Stephenson's £400 engine, which opened the world's first passenger railway between Stockton and Darlington in 1825, made the 14-mile journey again in July, to mark the railway's centenary. Making a good six miles an hour it led a procession of locomotives and rolling stock to show one hundred years of railway progress. Britain now had 20,314 miles of track, trains weighing 1,500 tons and engines costing £8,000 to build.

RIDER HAGGARD DIED

on May 14, after an illness of four and a half months. His first novel lost £50 ; his fourth, "King Solomon's Mines," made him a fortune. He was not only a famous novelist. He had been government official in South Africa, an ostrich farmer and a barrister, but as landowner of 360 acres in Norfolk he found his chief interest in farming, and he was knighted for agricultural services in 1919. "I trust," he wrote, "that should my novels be forgotten, my other books on Agriculture may still serve to keep my memory green."

77

THE PRINCE OF WALES IN AFRICA

With the sailing of H.M.S. Repulse from Portsmouth on March 28, 1925, the Prince of Wales began his 25,000 miles tour to Africa and South America. While Socialists nearly split on condemning or defending this £15,000 trip, South African cities were going gay with bunting, flowers and new paint. The Prince, welcomed at Cape Town by Boer General Hertzog, head of the Nationalists who had just come into power, left two days later for an eighty-day tour of the Union. He had given one thousand handshakes, and his arm was in a sling.

BY SEA —

REVIEWING TROOPS ——

on the pier at Capetown. Little more than a year before, when the "Repulse" anchored here, there had been marked anti-British prejudice. These feelings were eased by the Prince's visit.

AND LITTLE BLACK BOYS —

piccaninny-like pathfinders, lined up at Salisbury, in Southern Rhodesia.

— AND (LESS

the Prince travelled 20,000 miles in the "Repulse," exercising in a special "pulling boat" and on a squash rackets court built on the superstructure deck. The sailors cheered him and called him "a good sport."

THAT HAT

is worn by those who have the degree of Doctor of Law at Johannesburg University. It was given to the Prince in June. A University student posed as the Royal visitor, inspected the guard of honour, acknowledged the crowd's cheers, listened attentively to the address of welcome and entered the University. Then the real Prince arrived and the programme had to begin again.

HAPPILY) BY BOAT

Sitting in a narrow, dug-out craft paddled along the Zambesi River by four natives, he sat a little ill-at-ease; smiled broadly on reaching land.

QUEEN ALEXANDRA DIED

in November 1925, and was buried at Sandringham during a snowstorm. As a fair, Danish princess she had come to England more than sixty years before as the bride of Edward VII, then Prince of Wales. Queen Mother for fifteen years before her death, she had become popularly known as "Queen of the Roses," for roses were sold to help the hospitals on June 26 each year, "Alexandra Day," the day that had been chosen, in 1912, to commemorate her landing in England. In a special birthday message to the "Daily Express" in December 1924, she said: "How wonderful England is! Tell the people of Britain how grateful I am to them for thinking of me on my eightieth birthday."

80

HINDENBURG BECAME GERMANY'S PRESIDENT

on the death of President Ebert, the Socialist, in February 1925. Here is Germany's outstanding war hero, who had driven the Russian army out of Germany at the beginning of the War, and brought home his troops under the best possible conditions at the end of it; he is holding his field-marshal's staff on his way to church after reviewing troops in Potsdam. "Is it true, field marshal that when nervous you whistle?" asked a reporter. "Yes" said Hindenburg. "I have never heard you whistle" replied the reporter. Said Hindenburg, without a smile: "I never whistle."

and The Next Year—

Germany Entered The League —

Delegates from more than fifty nations attended the two-hour meeting at Geneva on September 10, when the Germans, under Dr. Stresemann, walked in to take their seats in the League Assembly. Here are Dr. Stresemann, Sir Austen Chamberlain, then Britain's Foreign Secretary, M. Briand of France and Dr. Schubert, German Foreign Office Secretary after the meeting.

SKIRTS WERE AT THEIR SHORTEST

They had reached the knee by the end of 1926. In speeches and newspaper articles, people denounced the immodesty of the new fashion. "Do grown-up married women wear their dress above the knee?" asked Judge Sir Alfred Tobin in January. "Yes, if they are slim" said a woman witness. "Do you mean to say one's grandmother would wear a short skirt" cried the judge. "What ridiculous nonsense!" Dressmakers complained, too, because only three yards of material were needed where formerly seven had been used.

HATS WERE "CLOCHE"

bell-like, fitting closely to the head because of the new shingled hair fashion. In the British Medical Journal a doctor wrote that he had noticed three cases in a fortnight of rash behind the ears among women wearing these hats. The space behind the ears must be ventilated, he warned; but the style still stayed popular.

AND—GENTLEMEN PREFERRED BLONDES

International best seller in 1926 was Anita Loos's chuckle-provoking "Gentlemen Prefer Blondes." Twenty-six years of age, married to American scenario writer John Emerson, this slight, wide-eyed brunette had written the first part of the book during a train journey, "just to while away the time."

Here is Anita Loos after arriving in London with her husband in August, to put on their play "The Whole Town's Talking." It was a moderate success. In October when the Lord Chamberlain refused to permit the performance of her play "The Fall of Eve," Anita Loos cabled to the "Daily Express": "The Lord Chamberlain is absolutely right. 'The Fall of Eve' is a very improper play and its production would undoubtedly undermine the morals of the British public."

THAT WAS THE YEAR OF THE CHARLESTON

the hectic, high-stepping rhythmic exercise that was promptly banned in many ballrooms to prevent accidents. On crowded dance floors, the side-kick steps of the Charleston meant torn stockings and barked shins. Doctors, too, condemned this side-kicking; they said it strained ligaments in the legs. The Charleston was described by an expert exponent as "an exaggeratedly syncopated waggle, impossible to interpret merely with the feet." In the autumn, a new and easier Charleston was introduced; the kicks had been abolished, the feet were now scarcely lifted from the floor. By the end of 1926, the tango was also coming into favour.

JAZZ was still causing great controversy, especially now that Gershwin had given the world "Rhapsody in Blue." Sir Landon Ronald attacked jazz in a wireless debate, saying of it: "We are inclined to revert to a barbaric taste and forget such a thing as beauty in the world." In April, Paul Whiteman's American jazz orchestra filled the Albert Hall before they began their English tour. That year, people hummed and whistled "Horsey! Keep Your Tail Up!" "Valencia" and Gershwin tunes from the show "Lady Be Good."

PRINCESS ELIZABETH WAS BORN

on April 21, 1926, and was christened Elizabeth Alexandra Mary at Buckingham Palace the following month. "Her Royal Highness and the infant Princess are making very satisfactory progress" said the official bulletin. The phrase "infant Princess" was a reminder of Queen Victoria's advice to the official who had referred to the birth of a royal baby. "Royal ladies" he was told "do not have babies; they have princes or princesses." First child to be born to the then Duke and Duchess of York, Princess Elizabeth was now, after the Prince of Wales and her father, heir to the Throne.

This group, taken at the christening, includes, from left to right: Duke of Connaught, Queen Mary, King George V, Duchess of York (with Princess Elizabeth), Duke of York, Countess of Strathmore, Earl of Strathmore and Princess Mary.

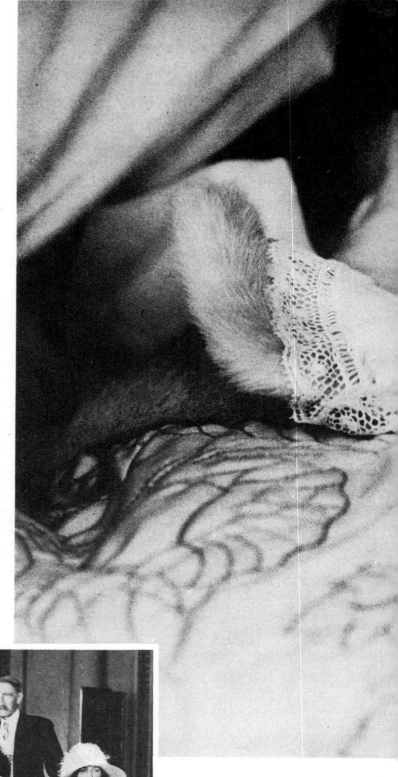

84

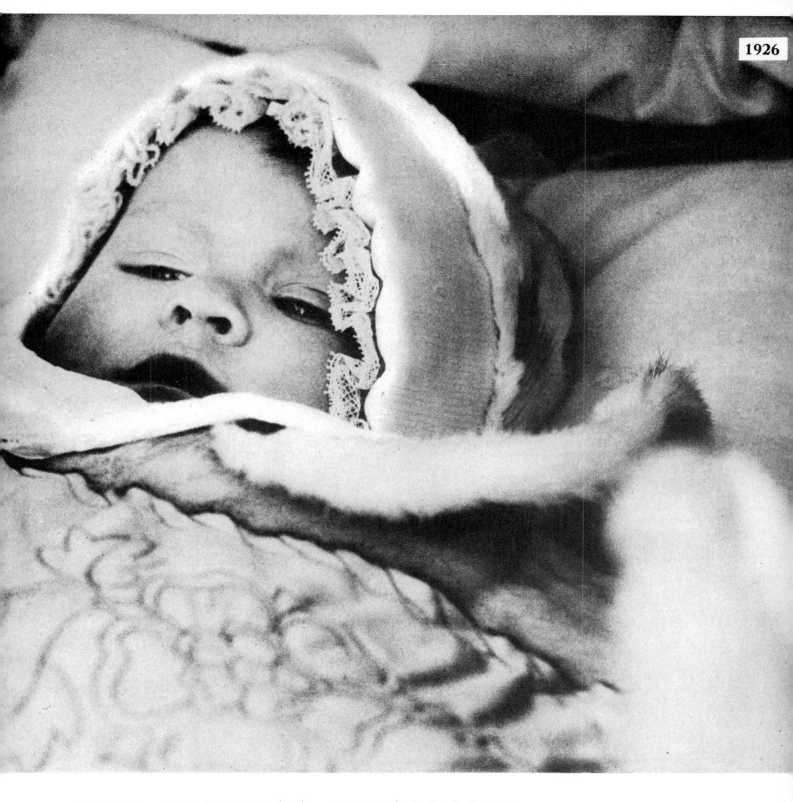

SHE HASN'T CHANGED MUCH, HAS SHE ?

She had blue eyes and weighed a little under average. All through her christening she cried lustily, but at six months she was a smiling, good-tempered child. She was said to take after her father in appearance, but had her mother's disposition.

IN 1926 WE WON THE ASHES

At the Oval, Kennington, England under A. P. F. Chapman met Australia in the fifth and deciding Test match of the 1926 series. Mainly owing to Mailey's googlies, England were all out in the first innings for 280 runs; Australia, owing to fine bowling by Larwood and Stevens, all out for 302. In the second innings, England made 436, and in three hours Australia were all out for 125. The last time England had won the Ashes at the Oval had been in 1912, and the teams fled as twenty thousand people ran on to the pitch to cheer them.

and Greyhound Racing Started

Fewer than two thousand spectators, more than half having been admitted free, watched Mistley win the first public greyhound race to be held in England, at Manchester Belle Vue track on July 24, 1926. This was the start of the sport that now draws 22,000,000 people each year to more than one hundred tracks all over Britain.

86

THEY CALLED THE ONE-WAY SYSTEM "GYRATORY"

in that year. This was Hyde Park Corner on the first day of "the new gyratory system of traffic control." Seventeen former streams of traffic had been merged into four.

Gyratory systems were not the only new traffic attractions for 1926. Covered-top "Generals" were running for the first time, not without criticism from Spartans.

One day a Mr. Cobham climbed into a plane

at Rochester, Kent, kissed his wife then waved and set off with A. B. Elliott, his mechanic, on a flight over an all-British air route to Australia. He wanted to show how Empire air-routes could be developed. He had made a 15,000 miles flight to India and back and a 17,000 miles flight to South Africa and back ; he said of his Australian flight : "This airplane job is quite an ordinary course of procedure."

THREE MONTHS LATER

he landed on the Thames at Westminster at the end of a 28,000 miles third Empire flight, Australia and back. Elliott was not with him. He had been killed by an Arab's bullet, fired as they flew over the desert on their way to the Persian Gulf. First person to greet Alan Cobham as the launch brought him ashore, was his wife ; then came Sir Samuel Hoare, Air Minister, to read out a message of congratulation from the King. In October, Mr. Cobham, air pioneer of Empire, was knighted for his services.

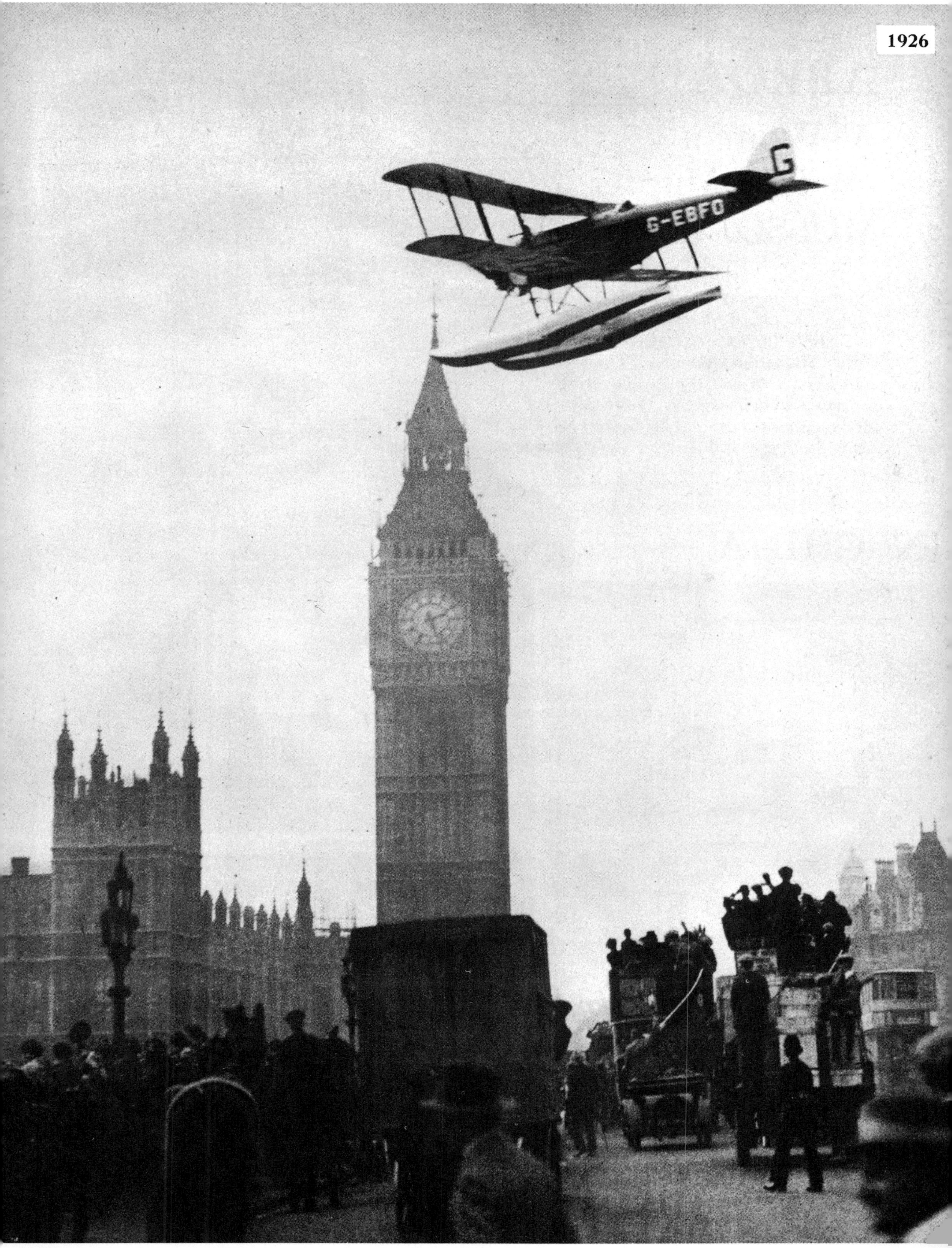
1926
G
G-EBFO

ABROAD —

A Woman tried to Murder MUSSOLINI

As Mussolini came out from the International Congress of Surgery in the Capitol, Rome, a woman stepped from the crowd, lifted a small pistol and fired, hitting Mussolini in the nose. The wound was slight. When the police arrested her, she gave her name as Violet Gibson, fifty-six years old daughter of the late Lord Ashbourne who had died in 1913. She was taken away to an asylum.

IN CHINA —

CHIANG KAI-SHEK, a thin, bald man who had proved himself a brilliant soldier, got from the Russian Government several million roubles to equip a revolutionary army, which, Russia thought would help make China a new Soviet. With this new Nationalist army, Chiang Kai-Shek began war in Southern China and at the end of 1926, entered Shanghai.

THE WORLD'S LOVER DIED

Holding a small, silver crucifix in his hand, Rudolph Valentino, handsome, dark athletic Italian who was the screen idol of millions of women, died suddenly in New York from peritonitis, at the age of thirty-one. His body was embalmed to lie in state in the gold room of a Broadway chapel. Forty publicity agents handled the funeral arrangements, 1,500 police officers were hired to line the route and in pouring rain, thousands of people, mostly women, cried and sobbed as the funeral cortege passed through the streets.

When he was growing a beard for one of his film parts, Valentino stood beside a goat, had his photograph taken and sent the picture to his friends with the note: "The one with the whiskers is the goat." Here he is, with his beard, when he stayed in London.

Below: lying in state in the Broadway chapel, with a friend, Eva Miller, praying beside the bronze coffin.

91

A. J. COOK led the Miners and the miners led the strike

Coal-mines had come under Government control towards the end of the War; in 1920 a twelve-day strike by the miners brought temporary wage increases. The following year, mines once again came under private ownership and miners were told that national rates of pay would stop and the pre-war system of paying according to districts would begin. They came out on strike for three months; but, receiving no support from the Government, went back to work under district rates of pay. As trade conditions became worse, coal-owners began to demand reduced wages and longer hours for miners. Arthur J. Cook, the miners' leader, eloquent speechmaker with a liking for slogans, gave miners the cry: "Not a minute on the day, not a penny off the pay."

Mr. Baldwin promised a subsidy to the coal industry while a Royal Commission investigated the problems, but eight months later, when the Commission, under Sir Herbert Samuel, issued their report, miners and owners rejected its findings. The Government refused to intervene until the miners and owners could reach agreement. At this stage, the country's Trade Union leaders, who had already advanced the theory that a general strike of all workers would be the best way to enforce the claims of any particular section of industry, threatened Mr. Baldwin. Unless the Government negotiated a settlement, they said, a general strike would be called at midnight, May 3, 1926. On May Day, 25,000 people took part in demonstrations at Hyde Park. Two days later the "Daily Mail" did not appear because the mechanical staff refused to print an article dealing with the crisis. Downing Street was informed at once. Hyde Park was closed to the public, and became the centre of London's milk supplies. The following night, Britain's trains, trams and buses came to a stop.

When this was done to a bus

which had been set on fire by strikers in South London, police protection was given to drivers. Barbed wire (seen below) was fixed over bus bonnets.

Volunteer Drivers were given Escorts

 ## "Society did its bit"

Lady Gisborough, Lady Malcolm (with frying pan) and Lady Louis Mountbatten (with pudding spoon), helping in the Hyde Park food kitchens.

1926

IT DID NOT LAST LONG

Troops organised food supplies, nearly half a million men enrolled as special constables, men and women everywhere volunteered for vital services and the Government published an official paper, "The British Gazette," as an antidote to wild rumour. On May 8, a two mile convoy of lorries, escorted by armoured cars, took food from the docks to Hyde Park; on May 10, 3,677 trains were being run by volunteers and on May 12, the cry came out: "Back to work!" The miners stayed out for seven months and went back in the end, defeated.

The British Gazette

Published by His Majesty's Stationery Office.

No. 1.   LONDON, WEDNESDAY, MAY 5, 1926.   ONE PENNY.

FIRST DAY OF GREAT STRIKE

Not So Complete as Hoped by its Promoters

PREMIER'S AUDIENCE OF THE KING

Miners and the General Council Meet at House of Commons

FOOD SUPPLIES

No Hoarding: A Fair Share for Everybody

MILK DISTRIBUTION

Control of Supplies in the Metropolis

LAW COURTS AT WORK

Judge on the Duty of the Public

G.P.O. SERVICES

Restrictions on Telegrams and Letters

THE KING RECEIVES THE PREMIER

HOLD-UP OF THE NATION

Government and the Challenge

NO FLINCHING

The Constitution or a Soviet

COMMUNIST LEADER ARRESTED

Mr. Saklatvala, M.P., Charged at Bow Street

SEQUEL TO MAY DAY SPEECH

THE "BRITISH GAZETTE" AND ITS OBJECTS

Reply to Strike Makers' Plan to Paralyse Public Opinion

REAL MEANING OF THE STRIKE

Conflict Between Trade Union Leaders and Parliament

THE OFFICIAL PAPER

under Winston Churchill, was published daily from May 5 until May 12. "The British Gazette," of only two pages, was the national news-sheet; the "Daily Express managed to appear every day, as a single sheet, printed and published by volunteer staffs. Below: A girl, unable to travel by bus, tram or train, gets a lift on a motor-cycle.

And its Editor 👉

PLEASE TAKE ME

FACES THAT YEAR

 A MISS JESSIE MATTHEWS

dark eyed, slightly built, one of a family of eleven children who had been brought up in Soho, arrived frightened but determined for an audition before theatre producer Andre Charlot. One hundred other girls were queued up, though only twenty-four were needed. "What do you mean by keeping me waiting?" demanded Jessie as Charlot came near, "I want my lunch." Amused, Andre Charlot turned to her and said: "Step out, you're engaged." Standing on an empty stage, she sang a simple little song into the microphone and a minute later, the wax record of her voice was played back to the critics. They liked it; Jessie Matthews was at the beginning of her stage career.

GERTRUDE EDERLE

On the morning of August 6, 1926, a sturdy, eighteen year old American girl plunged into the water at Cape Grisnez and 14 hours 42 minutes later walked ashore near Deal, the first woman to swim the English Channel. Gertrude Ederle became, in a few hours, the most publicised woman in the world. Only five swimmers, all men, had previously swum the Channel, and the record time had been the 16 hours 25 minutes of E. Tiraboschi in 1923. "Ten minutes after we swept round from Dover to Deal" said her trainer, "the tide turned. If we had been ten minutes later, no one could have swum against it." Gertrude's comment was: "It was worth doing to see how pleased Poppa is. He promised me a motor car when I did it."

FIRST SEEN AT WIMBLEDON IN 1927 —

Betty Nuthall, sixteen years of age, winner of the Junior Singles Championships 1924-26, played on the centre court at Wimbledon against the German tennis champion, pretty eighteen-year-old Cilli Aussem, and won the match. The following day she startled the lawn tennis world by beating Mrs. Mallory, eight times woman champion of the United States. "I just don't know how I did it" said Betty after the match. "It was the greatest surprise of my life. I did not expect to win." In those days she used to put her tongue in her cheek whenever she did anything particularly good or bad.

1927

CILLI AUSSEM

now married to the Italian count Fermo Murari della Corte Brae, was unable to play in international tennis during the next two years owing to serious eye trouble, but in 1931 she astonished everybody by winning both the English and the French women's championships.

MAJOR SEGRAVE DID 203 M.P.H.

Hurtling over Daytona Beach, Florida, in his 1,000 h.p. car "Golden Arrow," Major H.O.D. Segrave in white suit and helmet broke Captain Malcolm Campbell's previous world record of 174.22 m.p.h. by reaching an average speed of 203.79 m.p.h. Before the attempt, "Golden Arrow" was started up by compressed air and driven to the start of the nine-mile course. When the signal came "All clear!" Segrave started off in first gear at 73 m.p.h.; reached 132 m.p.h. in second and then went into top. Faster and faster went the car, becoming more and more difficult to hold in a straight line. Ten thousand spectators held their breath as a gust of wind sent the great car skidding towards the sea, ploughing through marking flags, then swerving back again as Segrave gained control. After the record had been broken, he was carried shoulder-high, back to his hotel. His wrists ached, he had burns, caused by the wind. He said: "I think we have put the world's speed record where it will stay for some considerable time to come." The following year, though, Malcolm Campbell at Daytona, travelled at 206.96 m.p.h.

The Owners of all these Top Hats

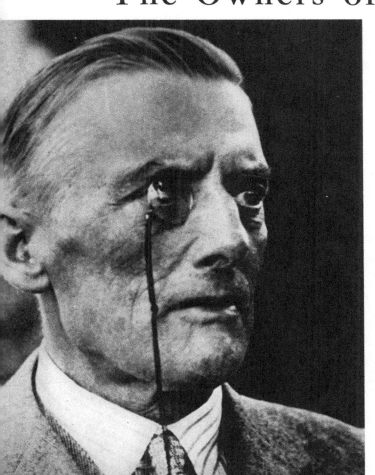

were looking at Mr. Frank Curzon's "Call Boy," the Derby favourite which won the race in 2 minutes 34 2/5 seconds—equal to the fastest time ever then recorded for the race. Mr. Curzon, so ill that he had difficulty in leading in his horse after its triumph, went home to bed soon after.

☞ 1927 WAS "AUSTEN'S" YEAR

Sir Austen Chamberlain, Britain's Foreign Secretary since 1924, made a world-wide impression by his vigorous speech on foreign policy at Geneva in September, when delegates of forty-seven nations met for the League of Nation's Assembly. Saying that this country could not increase her commitments towards the League, he said: "I yield to no one in my devotion to this great League of Nations but not even for this League of Nations will I destroy that smaller but older league of which my own country was the birthplace, and of which it remains the centre. . . . . Beware how you so draw tight the bonds, how you so pile obligation on obligation and sanction on sanction, lest at last you find you are not living nations but dead States."

ABROAD: Kaiser's sister marries ex-dish washer

Touched by the stories of 27-year-old Alexander Zoubkoff, poverty-stricken Russian refugee who had been dish-washer, sailor and circus-performer, the ex-Kaiser's sister, 61-year-old Princess Victoria of Schaumburg-Lippe, married him in November, 1927, much to the consternation of the German authorities. By this marriage she lost her brother's favour, most of her friends, her palace and fortune. Two years later, disillusioned, bankrupt, she died of pneumonia just when she was about to bring divorce proceedings against Zoubkoff, who was reported to be in love with a barmaid.

TROTSKY EXILED

Before his death, Lenin had warned the Russian Communists against Stalin, general secretary of the Party, but when Trotsky read out this message to the Communist leaders, Stalin shrugged his shoulders and said Lenin was not mentally responsible when he wrote his last will. The explanation was accepted, but Stalin deeply resented the matter having been brought up. In September, he denounced Trotsky's policy of World Revolution. "We have had enough of this idiotic slogan" he said. "Without the assistance of the outer world, Russia cannot exist." Foreign propaganda activity stopped, Stalin's views gained increasing sympathy and, in December, Trotsky was exiled to Turkestan and later banished from the Soviet Union.

SACCO & VANZETTI EXECUTED

The paymaster of an American shoe company was shot dead in April, 1920, by bandits who escaped with £3,750. Three weeks later, two Italians, Sacco, a shoemaker and Vanzetti, a fish-pedlar, were charged with the murder. Evidence was flimsy; 99 witnesses for the defence testified these men could not have been guilty. But America at that time was suffering from a "Red" scare and Sacco and Vanzetti held anarchist views. The case and its appeals dragged on for seven years; Madieros, a gangster, confessed to the crime, but in spite of world-wide protest, in August, 1927, the two men were electrocuted.

AT YPRES

Out of the ruins and desolation of 1918, when not one whole building had been left standing, had grown a new community. "Hellfire Corner," "Clapham Junction"—all the old familiar soldiers' landmarks were gone. To mark the scene of some of the Great War's grimmest fighting, the Menin Gate Memorial had been built in white Portland stone, engraved with the names of 58,600 British soldiers who lay in unknown graves. Field Marshal Lord Plumer opened the Memorial Gate in July 1927.

IN CHICAGO

After a fiercely fought election in which 5,000 police and 35 machine-gun squads were needed, eighteen-stone "Big Bill" Thompson became Mayor of Chicago with an 80,000 majority in a total vote of one million. His campaign had been run on an anti-British programme ; he promised to rid the school history books of alleged British propaganda ; and saying that Chicago's school superintendent had been appointed by influence from Buckingham Palace, used slogans such as : "Keep King George out of Chicago." Said the New York Evening Post : "The election of Mr. Thompson is little short of a national as well as a local disgrace." The New York Evening World, heading its leading article, "The Patriotic Swindle," wrote : "Mr. Thompson is a cheap, scheming politician of the low, cunning type." But his followers said he was the most misunderstood man on earth.

ANOTHER AMERICAN FACE

belonged to Charles Lindbergh, six-foot young man who flew out into the dark Newfoundland fog on May 20, to fly 3,500 miles across the Atlantic in an attempt to win a £5,000 prize offered for the first New York-Paris flight. Americans who had known of him as the "Lucky fool" because of previous air feats in that country, said pessimistically : "That's the last of him. He has tried too much." Only once before had the Atlantic been crossed in a non-stop flight—in 1919, when Alcock and Brown flew from Newfoundland to Ireland. But on Saturday May 21, tape machines clicked out the message : "Captain Lindbergh arrived at Le Bourget Airdrome at 10.15 p.m."

HIS PLANE

ARRIVED —

at Le Bourget Airdrome, Paris, after his 33½ hours flight, Lindbergh was so cold and numbed that he could not speak to the crowds that welcomed him. A few days later he flew to Croydon and more than 100,000 people waited to greet him. They burst through the fences as his plane landed and he sat for ten minutes in the cockpit while police cleared a way through the madly cheering mob. His first remark was : "Heaven help my machine."

HE GOT OUT

amid such storms of enthusiasm as had never before been known for any other popular visitor. He seemed dazed at the tumultuous welcome ; at first looked serious and almost glum, but gradually his features relaxed. He grinned and said : "This is worse than Le Bourget—or perhaps I should say better."

AND WHEN HE GOT BACK HOME—

He had the noisiest, craziest and most enthusiastic reception of all. New York was put out because President Coolidge, who had sent a warship to bring Lindbergh home, invited the airman to land at Washington and stay as guest at the White House for a day or two. New York's mayor said : "It is contrary to every tradition, since it is customary for distinguished visitors to go to New York first and to proceed to Washington later." When Lindbergh eventually got to New York from Washington, the city forgot its sulks. Nearly two million people gathered along the three mile route to and from the City Hall ; snowstorms of paper thrown from every window showered down on the procession and not even the entry of America into the Great War took up so much space in the newspapers next day as the return of Charles Lindbergh (now "Lindy" to everybody) to New York.

AS YOU CAN SEE "THE DOGS" CAUGHT ON

Prizes worth £40,000 were competed for during the summer of 1927, and more than 1,000 dogs were now registered to run on tracks controlled by the Greyhound Racing Association. In damp, dismal weather thirty thousand people flocked to the new greyhound course at Harringay on its opening night in September, and pitches were taken there by eight hundred bookmakers. All over the country, new tracks were being opened, and at the new White City Stadium there was room for 80,000 spectators. Charlie Munn, American millionaire who had first brought the electric hare to England, said to the "Daily Express" in December: "I believe so much in the future of greyhound racing that I have never taken a penny out of it. All my money is still in it and will remain there."

FIRST "CLASSIC" GREYHOUNDS

When the first greyhound Derby was run at the White City in October 1927, Mr. E. Baxter won all the prize money, for his three dogs Entry Badge, Ever Bright and Elder Brother came in first, second, and third. Other famous greyhounds of that time included Bonzo, Penny Bun and Duveneck, the trio that had helped introduce dog racing to this country. Before 1926, average price of a good dog had been about £20; to-day the average is £100 and dogs qualifying for the greyhound Derby are valued at £1,000 or more. Greatest dog of all has been Mick the Miller, winner of two Dog Derby's in succession.

THE COINAGE CHANGED

King George V approved the designs by George Kruger Gray for a new set of silver coins on November 3, 1927. For the first time since 1902, a new crown was to be issued from the Royal Mint. Once again, the Rose, Thistle and Shamrock appeared in the coinage. They had been absent since Queen Victoria's reign.

"OXFORD BAGS" AT THEIR WIDEST

were seen in the West End of London when a man, wanting to win a wager, walked out in trousers measuring forty-eight inches across each leg. The fashion of extra-wide trousers, begun in 1923, though still popular among undergraduates was now dying out generally, but trousers have never got back to the narrow widths of pre-war days.

PICCADILLY UP FOR THREE MONTHS

In the early morning of September 22, shopkeepers at the eastern end of Piccadilly looked grimly at a gang of roadworkers, with picks, shovels and drills, marching across the new, broad level roadway. Only thirty-six hours before, after having been closed since July 25, this part of Piccadilly had been opened to traffic, but now the authorities had decided to dig a bit up again to make an island site. Not till October 21, was the whole length of Piccadilly open to traffic once more. Trade losses were estimated at more than £20,000, but London sight-seers had been given a grand free show. Strube, in a "Daily Express" cartoon, showed an army of navvies marching along with drills on their shoulders and singing "Goodbye Picc-a-dil-ly!" while shopkeepers lined the route and cheered them as they went by.

FIRST AUTOMATIC PHONE

When an engineer knocked out a wedge between two cables at midnight on November 12, Holborn, first London automatic telephone exchange, switched over from the old to the new method of working. For some weeks after people said that the "auto-phones" did not get numbers at a fraction of the speed of the "Number Please" girls, but the Post Office answered that this was due to congestion on the lines; and the following year announced they were going to spend £25,000,000 to extend the automatic system. Here are some automatic meters in an exchange. Each subscriber has a meter on which his calls are registered; they are operated as soon as a call is answered and kept working till the call ends. For subscribers with poor eyesight, the Post office issued special dial phones (above) marked with large figures.

THE ARCOS RAID

Sir Wyndham Childs, then head of the special branch of the C.I.D., directed the police raid on 49 Moorgate Street, London headquarters of the Soviet trading company (Arcos) in May 1927. Every entrance to the building was guarded by six or more police. From 4.30 p.m. to 10.30 p.m. rooms were ransacked, safes broken open and various papers confiscated. Full facts of the raid and details of the documents found were never made public by the Government, but soon after diplomatic relations with the Soviet were broken off and most of the officials of Arcos left the country.

THE NEW FORD

was revealed to the public in December and for the first time the Ford car was not the cheapest on the British market. The new two-seater sold at £145; Morris was making a two-seater for £142 10 0. For five years, at a cost of £20,000,000, Henry Ford had been planning a new model because the car which made him famous, the Ford "Tin Lizzie," did not appeal to women buyers. They disliked driving in a car which had been the subject of so many jokes. However, jokes or no jokes, sales of the old Ford model passed the fifteen million mark that year.

TWO FACES THAT YEAR

Lion Feuchtwanger, a German Jew, was author of the most discussed novel of 1927, "Jew Suss." Novelist Arnold Bennett had made it popular in England. "It is already a matter of history" said Feuchtwanger, during a visit to London in the November, "that it was Arnold Bennett in the Evening Standard who first made the book widely known." In America, "Jew Suss" appeared under the title "Power." "We like one-word titles" said the publisher, "We shall call his next book "Success". Feuchtwanger's next book, published in 1927, was "The Ugly Duchess."

JOHN BUCHAN

Scottish writer and historian, author of "The Thirty-Nine Steps" and now Lord Tweedsmuir, Governor General of Canada, was elected Unionist M.P. for the Scottish Universities in June, 1927. The following month he made his maiden speech in Parliament, attacking Viscount Cave's proposals for reforming the House of Lords. It was a brilliant speech, the best, said politicians, since Lord Birkenhead's maiden speech of 1906.

FIRST WOMAN FLYER
ACROSS THE ATLANTIC

Miss Amelia Earhart —

"I am the proudest woman in the whole world" said America's "Miss Lindy," 29-year-old Amelia Earhart when, with Wilmer Stultz, pilot, and "Slim" Gordon, mechanic, she landed at South Wales on June 18 after a 1,900-miles non-stop flight from Newfoundland in the triple-engined seaplane "Friendship." First woman to cross the Atlantic, she said to reporters: "I would sooner fly the Atlantic ten times than face all this publicity and fuss again." Then she went off to London to buy some clothes.

HOW WOULD YOU DRESS A 'TOMBOY' STYLE?

Here she is with Lord Astor at the Derby. That was four years later: little more than a week before she had again flown from Newfoundland on the first solo Transatlantic flight ever undertaken by a woman, and after sixteen hours had landed in a field near Londonderry. This time she said: "I am very glad to have come across successfully but I am sorry indeed that I did not make France." Then she went shopping once more.

Another Great Flight
First EAST-to-WEST

Two Germans, Captain Koehl, Baron von Huenefeld and an Irishman, Major Fitzmaurice, set out from Dublin in a German Junkers monoplane on Thursday morning, April 12, in an effort to make the first east to west Atlantic flight. They were forced down on a lonely, desolate island north of Newfoundland, but relief planes rescued them, took them to Quebec (above), and then to New York. (Here they are in that city: Capt. and Mrs. Koehl, Major and Mrs. Fitzmaurice, monocled Baron von Huenefeld with Patricia Fitzmaurice). They had only a quiet reception when they first arrived back at Plymouth. Wrote the "Daily Express: "In the conquest of the air and the sea there is rivalry, but no racial prejudice or jealousy. Full justice has not been done to the heroic effort." That same day, the Royal Aero Club invited the airmen to an official reception.

—BUT THIS FLIGHT FAILED

On the thirteenth of March, Captain Hinchcliffe and the Hon. Elsie Mackay, third daughter of Lord Inchcape, set off secretly on an Atlantic flight attempt. A week before, when the "Daily Express" had published news of the proposed flight, Elsie Mackay had said to reporters : "The report is quite unfounded. I have no intention of accompanying Capt. Hinchcliffe." Even after the plane had left, a Mr. Sinclair was stated to be the passenger, but the next day, Mr. Sinclair was seen in London. The "Daily Express" had been right, but why the flyers kept their flight so secret nobody ever found out ; they were never heard of again.

That Year, the Year of the FLAPPER VOTE

perky Ellen Wilkinson, copper-coloured hair M.P., won a triumph in December by securing from the authorities permission for women members of the House to have meals in the Strangers' Dining Room, which till then had always been reserved for men. For this feat, the bachelor M.P.'s gave her a New Year gift of an automatic gas cooker. Early in the year she had supported the Equal Franchise Bill which gave the vote to one and a half million women, between the ages of twenty-one and twenty-five years of age. "I hope that every member of the House" she said, "will realise that we are doing at last a great act of justice to the women of the country."

117

MANY FAMOUS PEOPLE

LORD HAIG

Commander of the British Forces in France during the War died in London, in January, at the age of sixty-six. His funeral procession, more than a mile long, went to Westminster Abbey, then to Waterloo Station, where the coffin was entrained for Scotland for the burial at Bemersyde, the late Earl's home. Pall bearers included Marshal Foch and seven British Field Marshals; the then Prince of Wales, Duke of York and Prince Henry followed the cortege.

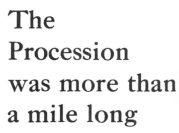

The Procession was more than a mile long

Once when on five days' leave in England, Haig spent the whole time quietly at home with his wife and declined an invitation to see the King at Buckingham Palace. The following year, after a visit to the troops in France, King George V wrote to Haig: "It is especially pleasing to me to find that the absolute confidence I have in you is shared throughout your command."

DIED IN 1928

LORD OXFORD

last of the great Gladstonians, Prime Minister from 1908-1916, connected with the Liberal party for forty years till he gave up the leadership in 1926, died in February. Here are Lord and Lady Oxford and Asquith with their son Anthony Asquith. When Lord Oxford was criticised, his favourite answer was: "They say: what say they? . . . . Let them say!"

☛ AND ELLEN TERRY

one of the world's greatest actresses, chiefly famous for her Shakespearian roles in which she had played with Sir Henry Irving (left), died at Small Hythe, Kent, in July. On the day of her funeral, the country roads for miles around were packed with cars and along the hundred yards of road between her house and the church, stood men in summer flannels and coloured ties, women in gay summery dresses; for Ellen Terry had said; "No funeral gloom, my dears, when I am gone."

ALSO DIED —

THOMAS HARDY

novelist, who all his life had been associated with the Wessex country and who showed in his writings, humour, psychology and dialect of the country, died in January, 1928. His body was cremated, the ashes buried in Poets' Corner, Westminster Abbey, and his heart buried in the parish churchyard near Dorchester.

MRS. PANKHURST

head Suffragette, leader of the Woman's Suffrage Movement, who had been imprisoned more than half a dozen times for her activities, including inciting to riot, window breaking, assault and complicity in a bomb outrage on Lloyd George's house, died at the age of sixty-eight in June.

"LITTLE TICH"

stage name of Henry Relph, the dwarf comedian who had been on the music hall stage for nearly fifty years, and at the height of his popularity was earning £450 a week, died in February almost penniless. "If ever you become top of the bill in the variety profession" he once said "you will be amazed at the number of poor relatives you will have to help."

17 WERE DROWNED —

Soon after 6 a.m. on Thursday, November 15, in blinding rain the crew of the lifeboat at Rye Harbour, Sussex, sailed out into a south-westerly gale to answer distress signals from the Latvian steamer "Alice." Five minutes later, a telephone message to the village reported that the Latvians had been saved by another steamer. The lifeboat could not be recalled. At half-past ten, watchers on the shore saw her capsize and a few hours later, bodies began to be washed ashore. All seventeen of the crew had been drowned. Since then no lifeboat has been kept at Rye.

HIS DEATH ☞ SHOOK LONDON

Alfred Lowenstein, Belgian financier, who had, it was estimated, made £14,000,000 in eighteen months, stepped out of his airplane while travelling from Croydon to Brussels and was drowned in mid-Channel. At the Stock Exchange next day, dealers refused to handle stocks in which he had been interested; there were heavy falls in shares. A fortnight later his body was found; but whether his death was suicide or accident, never became known.

121

POLICE "SPY-HOLE" BUILT

Soundproof, with slits in the wall like the arrow holes in medieval castles, a solid granite conning tower in direct telephone contact with Scotland Yard was put up in Trafalgar Square in January.

ANOTHER WOMAN CHANNEL-SWIMMER

"Thank God it's over" said Ivy Hawke, 25-year-old swimming instructress of Surbiton, after making the first successful Channel swim of 1928, in August. This was her third attempt; she had landed at Dover from Cape Grisnez after swimming for nineteen hours sixteen minutes.

In the "Spy-hole," which has steel doors and is considered to be impregnable, police officers can look-out on demonstrations without being seen, and are able to call up police reserves immediately, in case of threatened riots in the Square.

TWO AMERICANS—

Herbert Hoover, engineer, chief administrator of a £5,000,000 fund for research in pure science, and, as Secretary of Commerce, a super-salesman for American goods, was chosen as candidate for President by the Republicans in 1928. In his acceptance speech—the year before the great business slump—he said: "We in America to-day are nearer to the final triumph over poverty than ever before in the history of any land."

Frank Billings Kellogg, who had been U.S. Ambassador to Great Britain 1923-25, worked with M. Briand of France on a pact "to outlaw war" and in 1928, this peace pact was signed by fifteen principal nations of the world.

123

KING GEORGE V's ILLNESS

In December King George V was seriously ill with lung trouble. A month before, on a rainy, chilly day, he had attended the Cenotaph Armistice Day service, and a few days later had gone to bed suffering from a cold, with slight fever. "Old Kate," who had often sold him a race-card at Epsom on Derby Day, was among those who came to Buckingham Palace to hear news of his illness.

THESE PEOPLE ARE
LOOKING AT THIS ☞

Special prayers for King George V were said in churches all over the country on Sunday December 2. The Prince of Wales, hunting in Africa, cut short his tour and raced home to London. His father's first words to him were: "Well, David, did you get that lion?" All through December, crowds waited for bulletins to be posted up outside Buckingham Palace.

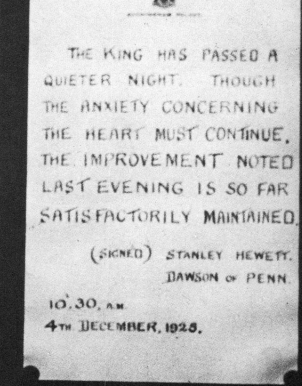

THE KING HAS PASSED A QUIETER NIGHT. THOUGH THE ANXIETY CONCERNING THE HEART MUST CONTINUE, THE IMPROVEMENT NOTED LAST EVENING IS SO FAR SATISFACTORILY MAINTAINED.

(SIGNED) STANLEY HEWETT.
DAWSON OF PENN.

10.30 A.M.
4TH DECEMBER, 1928.

Well Again

On January 23, 1929, appeared the most satisfactory bulletin of the whole illness. King George V, it said, was to be moved to the sea. The next month, lying in an ambulance car with blinds drawn up so that he could be seen by people lining the route, he was taken for convalescence to Bognor, and in July, well again, he drove through London with the Queen, in an open carriage.

THAMES FLOODS DROWN FOURTEEN

Ninety - miles - an - hour winds, piling up an exceptionally high tide in a river already raised above its normal level by flood water, made the Thames burst its banks in January, 1928. Fifty yards of the embankment gave way at Westminster, water poured into hundreds of houses and, almost in their beds, fourteen people were drowned. "The Thames floods are a sheer disgrace to the capital and to all the authorities concerned "wrote the "Daily Express." "In this imperial city, people were drowned as defencelessly as though London were a river village in the interior of China."

Tate Gallery Pictures Spoilt

Fifteen thousand of Turner's water colour paintings and sketches were included in the pictures, worth more than £1,500,000, spoilt by flood water pouring into the cellars of the Tate Gallery in Millbank, Westminster.

Houses of Parliament, Lambeth Palace, Tower of London, and Woolwich Arsenal were all flooded in January 1928. Boats were carried by the flood water over river walls; roadways were torn up and at Westminster, where sandbags were hurriedly piled up to cover breaches in the embankment, more than 500 telephone lines were put out of order. One thousand extra police were brought on duty to keep people away from this danger area.

25 KILLED IN WOODEN COACHES

In head-on collision, an excursion train packed with five hundred holiday-makers, crashed into a parcels train outside Bank Top station, Darlington, just before midnight on June 27. Wooden coaches of the excursion train were telescoped and thrown ripped open on the lines. Blame for this disaster, in which 25 were killed and 45 seriously injured, was placed on the driver of the parcels train who had misread a signal.

THESE TWO WERE LABOUR

in those days. Sir Oswald Mosley, who entered Parliament as a Conservative, became an Independent, then went over to Labour, and in 1929 held cabinet rank as chancellor of the duchy of Lancaster, followed his leader, Mussolini, in exchanging Socialism for Fascism. MacDonald, then head of the Labour party had yet to become head of a National government of Socialists, Liberals and Conservatives. In October, 1928, they both went to Berlin to speak at a congress on International Discussion.

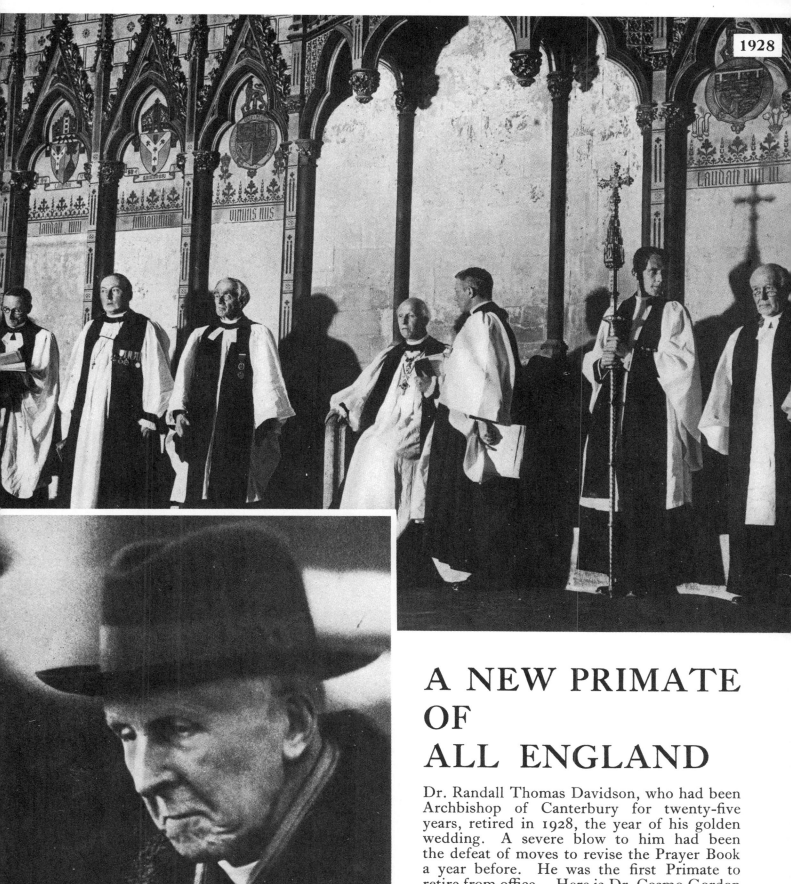

A NEW PRIMATE OF ALL ENGLAND

Dr. Randall Thomas Davidson, who had been Archbishop of Canterbury for twenty-five years, retired in 1928, the year of his golden wedding. A severe blow to him had been the defeat of moves to revise the Prayer Book a year before. He was the first Primate to retire from office. Here is Dr. Cosmo Gordon Lang who succeeded him. Scotsman, bachelor, seventh son of a seventh son, the new Primate, described by a bishop as "first-class orator, second-class preacher," was enthroned in December at Canterbury Cathedral.

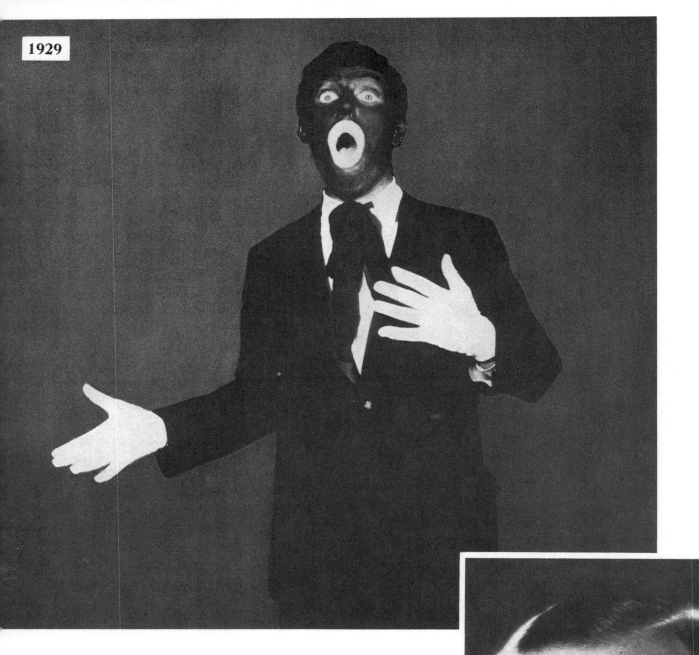

TALKIES BEGAN

"The Jazz Singer" was the first feature-length talking film, though its sound was mostly all synchronised music. Black-faced comedian Al Jolson sang six songs and also spoke a few lines. Just before recording a number, he had said, on the spur of the moment: "Come on Ma, listen to this." American audiences stood up and cheered at the spoken dialogue; this, they said, was the death of the silent movies. In England, critics said it was a freak, that the silent film would always be the real cinema. Jolson's next film, however, was a riot. "The Singing Fool" set up new attendance records all over the country in 1929, and got everybody whistling, humming or singing its song-hit, "Sonny Boy."

"BITTER SWEET"

Slick, American farces were being shown on the London musical stage in 1929. There had been little or no sentiment for a long while, and Noel Coward believed that a new romantic operetta would be a great success. Listening to a German orchestral record of "Die Fledermaus," in the early autumn of 1928, made him think of uniforms, bustles, chandeliers and gas-lit cafes—clues which gave him the setting for his operetta. The following months he worked on story and musical score. Sitting in a taxi during a twenty-minutes' traffic jam, he thought out the waltz "I'll See You Again." Manchester saw "Bitter Sweet" first, then London ; so successful was it that in the autumn of 1929, with Evelyn Laye as leading lady (right), "Bitter Sweet" was put on in New York.

131

LABOUR GOVERNMENT AGAIN

With unemployment figures well over the million mark, Labour's promises to end "misery, hunger and starvation within three weeks of coming into office" appealed to nearly 8½ million people who voted for them in the 1929 General Election. The Conservatives were defeated. Ramsay MacDonald took office in June as head of a Labour Government. Here is his Cabinet at No. 10 Downing Street :— Left to right : (standing) George Lansbury, A. V. Alexander, Sir C. Trevelyan, Margaret Bondfield, Lord Thomson,* T. Shaw, Arthur Greenwood, N. E. Buxton (Lord Noel-Buxton), W. Graham,* W. Adamson,* (sitting) J. R. Clynes, Lord Parmoor, J. H. Thomas, Philip Snowden* (later Viscount), J. Ramsay MacDonald,* Arthur Henderson,* Lord Passfield, Lord Justice Sankey, W. Wedgwood Benn. Those marked with a star are now dead.

"THE GOOD COMPANIONS"

"Mr. J. B. Priestley has written a long, leisurely and very lively novel after an old pattern, the picaresque, which will always, I imagine, be popular. It is the pattern of Don Quixote, The Canterbury Tales, Tom Jones, The Pickwick Papers . . . ." So wrote the "Daily Express" Book Critic in August 1929, when Priestley's 270,000 word book "The Good Companions" was published. Thirty-six years old, a burly humorous Yorkshireman, Priestley had been writing at 17 a weekly page for a Bradford paper. After the War, he had gone to Cambridge and in his third year there, married. "That meant I had to find a job" he said. "I decided to be a University extension lecturer, but at the last moment I changed my mind." He came to London as a literary free-lance. He had very little money. For a year, often working all day and far into the night, he was writing "The Good Companions." In little more than six months it had sold 95,000 copies here and 90,000 in America.

ABROAD:
BRITISH TROOPS LEAVE GERMANY

The last of five thousand troops who had been occupying the Rhineland since the War moved out of Wiesbaden in December, 1929, to the music of "Auld Lang Syne."

Thousands of Germans looked on and cheered. From the masthead by the entrance to General Headquarters, a tattered, weatherstained Union Jack that had been there ever since the first soldier marched into the Rhine area, was hauled down and taken away. Britain's long watch on the Rhine had ended.

GERMANY'S FOREIGN MINISTER DIED

Stout, bald, thick-necked Gustav Strese-mann, son of a Berlin beer merchant and a great statesman who had been Germany's foreign minister since 1923, died from a stroke in October. At his own wish, he was buried in Luisenstadt Parish Church-yard, in the centre of Berlin's city slums. King George V, in a message to the German ambassador said that he regarded Strese-mann's death a loss, not only to Germany, but to the whole of Europe. In 1926 Stresemann had shared the Nobel Peace Prize with M. Briand of France. Since the War he had worked consistently for peace in Europe and the rebuilding of Germany.

A Year before, he had signed the Treaty

which was to outlaw war—the Kellogg Peace Pact—in Paris. His great moment, however, had been the signing of the Locarno Treaty (right), in which Germany, France, Belgium and Britain had agreed that all disputes should be settled by peaceful means. "The deter-ioration of international relations in Europe" said Anthony Eden, in 1933, "dated from the death of Herr Stresemann."

IN INDIA:

An attempt on the life of Lord Irwin, as Lord Halifax was then, failed in December. On a 30-foot high embankment, a bomb exploded beneath the train that was bringing the Viceroy and his wife to their home in New Delhi. Part of the line was torn away, two carriages were damaged, but the train was not derailed and nobody was hurt.

IN ITALY:

the fifty-nine year old difference between Italy and the Vatican was settled in February with the signing of a treaty by Mussolini and representatives of the Holy See. Since 1870, when Papal troops surrendered to the armies of Victor Emmanuel, each Pope had considered himself a "prisoner" in an unfriendly State. The treaty established a new half-mile square European State around the Vatican. No longer would the Pope need to consider himself a "prisoner."

AND IN AMERICA— SLUMP!

Charles E. Mitchell, chairman of New York's great National City Bank, said in the first week of October : "Markets generally are now in a healthy condition. The last six weeks have done an immense amount of good by shaking down prices." On Thursday October 24, as soon as the Stock Exchange opened, brokers saw at once that prices were being shaken down much more than was good for them. Hundreds of thousands of shares were being thrown on the market, causing a panic, and by noon that day Mitchell met the rest of New York's bankers who agreed to spend fifty million pounds right then, to help keep up prices. The desperate remedy worked ; when the Stock Exchange closed, prices were fairly steady. The following Tuesday though, not even the bankers could stop Wall Street's panic. Sixteen million shares were put on the market, millions of pounds of paper profits disappeared, and in the next few days newspapers began publishing regular reports of suicides. The great American slump brought on by over production, artificial commodity prices and too much credit had begun.

Meanwhile in England—

HATRY CRASHED

Shares of seven companies controlled by fifty-year-old City financier, Clarence Hatry, had been falling early in September, and at the end of the third week these companies, valued at more than £10,000,000, collapsed. Hatry was arrested on charges of fraud. The following year Mr. Justice Avory sentenced him to fourteen years' imprisonment. After listening to Hatry's defence, the judge said: "It is nothing more or less than the threadbare plea of every clerk or servant who robs his master and says that he hoped to repay the money before his crime was discovered by backing a winner."

THESE CHILDREN'S CLOTHES

were left in a Paisley cinema by their panic-stricken wearers, who rushed to the window to get out after somebody had called out : "Fire !" On the last day of 1929 five hundred children were watching a cowboy film when a reel caught alight in the operator's box. Smoke filled the hall ; in Britain's worst cinema panic, the children, many of them little more than babies, rushed shrieking to the exits. All those who fell were trampled on and in the struggle to leave the building sixty-nine were killed, thirty-seven injured.

CLOUDBURST AT ASCOT

Just as the crowd were cheering The Macnab's victory in the Royal Hunt Cup at Ascot on June 18, a flash of forked lightning, followed by thunder and drenching rain, turned the meeting into a morass. Men and women fought for shelter, summer dresses were ruined, wide-brimmed hats flopped over their wearer's faces. A sign went up that had not been seen at Ascot for nearly a century: "Racing abandoned."

1930

LANSBURY LIDO OPEN

George Lansbury, then First Commissioner of Works, arranged for public mixed bathing in Hyde Park and at 4.30 p.m., on June 16, men and women bathers plunged for the first time together into the Serpentine. First woman in was 21-year-old Kathleen Murphy, of Pinner, who had arrived at the gate at five o'clock that morning. She was given a medal by Alfred Rowley, secretary of the Serpentine Swimming Club.

THAT YEAR LORD BIRKENHEAD DIED

Son of an estate agent, of Birkenhead, Frederick Edwin Smith had won a scholarship in classics and went from his local grammar school to Oxford. He graduated in Law, was called to the Bar at Grays Inn, and practising as a barrister in London soon made a big reputation for his handling of commercial cases. By 1914 he was earning £30,000 a year at the Bar. He was as successful in politics as he was in law, but his many activities caused overwork which brought on his premature death when he was 58. He was made a peer in 1919 when he became Lord-Chancellor.

HIS CIGARS WERE FAMOUS

Just as Winston Churchill is famous for his hats, Lord Birkenhead was famous for his cigars. Once, in Halifax, he entered a barber's and said: "They tell me I can't get a shave this afternoon because of early closing." He could if he kept quiet about it, said the barber. Birkenhead had the shave but told the barber when it was over: "As you're not allowed to shave, I'll not pay you any money." Instead he gave the barber two cigars.

Birkenhead's studied insolence often offended people. In a county court case, the judge, sympathising with a boy claiming compensation for blindness, kept muttering: "Poor boy, poor boy." He instructed police officers to stand the boy on a chair so that the jury could see. "Why not pass him round the jury box?" suggested "F. E." "A most improper remark" snapped the judge. "Provoked by a most improper suggestion" retorted "F. E." Furious, the judge shouted: "You are extremely offensive," getting the reply: "The only difference between us is that I am trying to be and you can't help it."

1930
WAS A TRIUMPHANT YEAR FOR WOMEN

First there was —

"AMY"

On May 24, after a lone flight of 9,900 miles from England, Amy Johnson, who eighteen months before had been a typist in a London office, stepped out of a battered and patched airplane at Port Darwin, Australia. She flung off lifebelt and goggles and began to tidy her hair with a comb before making her way through the cheering crowd of white people, Chinese, Japanese, Malays, Filipinos and Maltese for the official reception at Government House. She said : "Tell England, my father and mother, and the rest of the world that I am here safe and sound and so happy to have reached my goal. I have received no offers of marriage—and you may call me 'Johnny'."

1930

THEN THERE WAS "BETTY"

Not for twenty-seven years had Britain won any lawn tennis singles title in America. Then in August, Betty Nuthall, playing without stockings in a white dress with red band round her hips, beat Mrs. L. A. Harper, left-handed player from California, 6-1, 6-4; so winning the American women's singles tennis championship. Later, with Sarah Palfrey, she shared the doubles championship, too. Betty was given the Cup and a great bouquet of American Beauty roses. She was nervous; could only say: "Thank you very much."

CUPS FOR
DIANA FISHWICK

19-year-old Broadstairs girl who had never played in a golf championship event before. She defeated Glenna Collett, American champion, and so gained the British women's open golf championship.

WINIFRED BROWN

flying against eighty-seven other competitors over a 753-miles course, won the King's Cup Air Race. Sir Philip Sassoon gave her the cup.

AND A MEDAL FOR MARJORIE FOSTER

first woman to win the King's Prize at Bisley. Against ninety-nine men, she made 280 points out of a possible score of 300.

1930

RHINELAND EVACUATED

Thousands of Germans watched, stolid and silent, as the Tricolour of France was hauled down from the Castle Tower in Mainz, on Monday morning June 30, and French troops made their last march through the Rhineland town. Two hours later, General Guillaumat, commander-in-chief of the French Army in the Rhineland, followed across the frontier with his staff officers. At last the Rhineland was free of all Allied troops, the British having left in the previous year (Page 133). Joyfully, German garrison police marched in to occupy the barracks.

HITLER
WON THE ELECTIONS

Representatives of twenty-seven parties had been seeking election to the Reichstag, but the main conflict was between Communists and Fascists who each wanted to secure enough seats to make a Centre Government impossible. Results caused a sensation all over the world. Hitler's Fascist party, the National Socialists, who had gained only 12 seats at the previous election, this time had 107 seats. Hitler, now only a short step from being Germany's dictator, was not entitled to sit in the Reichstag. He was not a German—he had been born in Austria. Here he is with his chief of staff, Doctor Goebbels, acknowledging cheers from his followers. He said in 1930: "I wish to capture the soul of Germany by constitutional means."

IN SPAIN—

A REVOLUTION THAT FAILED

Spanish government censors clamped down on outgoing news reports in mid-December. Martial law had been proclaimed throughout Central and Northern Spain following an army rebellion at the garrison town of Jaca, near the French frontier. For many years there had been discontent with King Alfonso's rule and Republican propaganda had been intensive. Jaca's revolt was the signal for an outbreak of riots all over Spain. For many weeks there were constant battles between workers and police ; students on the roof of Madrid's Medical Faculty threw down stones on civil guards. Even after the arrest of Republican leaders and the quelling of riots, Spain still seethed with unrest.

CAROL KING AGAIN

Prince Carol of Rumania, unhappily married to Princess Helene, had renounced his rights to the throne in 1926 so that he could live in exile with full-lipped, red-haired Magda Lupescu, pretty half-Jewess with whom he had fallen in love. But when his hard-headed mother, Queen Marie, was temporarily out of the country, Carol flew to Bucharest in June, pushed his young son Michael, who had succeeded him, off the throne and became Carol II. By 485 votes to 1, the National Assembly accepted him as king.

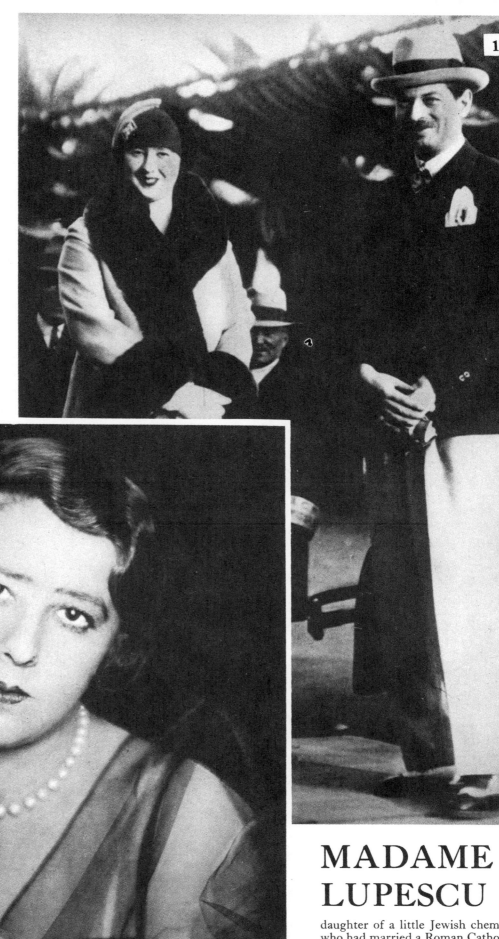

1930

MADAME LUPESCU

daughter of a little Jewish chemist who had married a Roman Catholic girl in Vienna, met Carol while he was on a vacation. Though already married to an army officer, Lupescu got a divorce when Carol told her how much he loved her.

GANDHI IN LONDON

Gandhi, wizened ascetic who wished to lead India's 350 million people away from the British Crown into complete independence, in May was arrested at dead of night at his camp near Surat, India. He had led a general agitation against British rule; boycotting foreign cloth, publicly making salt in defiance of the Salt Laws, and staging a movement of "civil disobedience without malice." For the rest of 1930, while he was in prison, the Government used extraordinary repressive measures to fight this civil disobedience movement. Hundreds were killed, thousands injured in riots and police attacks. At the end of the following January, Gandhi was released and in the September he came to London for Round Table conferences. All through his visit, he wore loin-cloth, white shawls and sandals.

"ANNABELLA" BEGAN

her film career in earnest when she appeared in a silent French film with synchronised music, "Sous les Toits de Paris." With English sub-titles it was shown in London in December. Directed by Rene Clair (left), it pictured the underworld life of Paris and was considered by critics to be one of the best films of 1930.

THE "KING" OF LUNDY

Martin Coles Harman, City financier who started as an office boy and worked his way up to the control of companies worth £14,000,000, bought the 1,000-acre island of Lundy, in the Bristol Channel and claimed that it was another State, not subject to the Crown. Its fifty inhabitants paid no rates or taxes in their small independent "kingdom." Harman was their king ; but in 1930 he was charged under the Coinage Act, 1870, for issuing illegal coins, just for Lundy, known as puffins and half-puffins (below). Lundy Islanders also had their own special stamp. Harman was fined £5 and 15 guineas costs. He lost his appeal.

SIR HENRY SEGRAVE KILLED

On Friday the 13th of June, after running perfectly along the marked course on Lake Windermere and achieving a new world's record of 98.76 m.p.h., Segrave's 4,000 h.p. motor-boat Miss England II, travelling at 103 m.p.h., suddenly leaped high in the air and fell upside down on the water. Segrave and a mechanic, Halliwell, were killed.

HIS BOAT 👉

Miss England II had hit a floating branch or perhaps a bottle thrown carelessly in the water by some holiday visitor. A head-on blow at more than 100 m.p.h. meant a force of impact equivalent to pressure of 1.4 tons to the square inch. Chief Engineer Wilcocks, only survivor of the disaster, said that on the third run, when Segrave knew the record had been broken, Miss England II moved much faster than on the other two runs. "Suddenly" he said, "I felt a dull thud. Immediately afterwards, the boat lifted and dipped."

THE LITTLE WHITE FIGURE BATTING IS—
BRADMAN

—playing in the 3rd Test Match at Leeds in July. Don Bradman, young Australian who only a few years before had been a farm lad at Bowral, near Sydney, made 334 runs before he was caught out by Duckworth. His 288th run caused such terrific enthusiasm among the crowds watching, that play had to be stopped for several minutes till the noise died down. With this run he smashed R. E. Foster's record highest individual innings of 287, scored at Sydney in 1903.

As the players struggled for stumps at the end of the 5th Test, ten thousand people rushed madly across the ground to get near the pavilion. Bradman had broken seven records during the Test series and Australia had regained the Ashes.

153

CARNERA

6-foot-10-inch heavyweight boxer who, little more than a year before, had been just a poorly-paid carpenter, came to London in December to fight Reggie Meen. At his hotel, he needed two beds placed together to give him comfortable rest. He wore size 16 in shoes, 21-inch collars and jackets measuring 58 inches round the chest. At the Albert Hall he won his fight after $4\frac{1}{2}$ minutes, then went off to a dance. "Poor Reggie Meen," he said, "I am sorry for him—but what could I do? I was glad when the referee stopped the fight."

"SHAMROCK V" BEATEN

Sir Thomas Lipton had spent nearly £1,500,000 trying to bring back to Britain the Cup that had been won, eighty-three years before, by the United States yacht "America" in a race off the Isle of Wight. In "Shamrock V" against Vanderbilt's yacht "Enterprise," he made his fifth attempt in September. He failed to bring back the "elusive old mug."

But Sir Thomas Lipton got a Cup

from Mayor Walker of New York, as a tribute to his sportsmanship. Americans all over the country had subscribed for it.

PRINCESS MARGARET ROSE

second child of the Duke and Duchess of York (now King and Queen), was born at Glamis Castle on August 21, the first Royal child to be born in Scotland for more than three hundred years. "I looked into the cot" said J. R. Clynes, then Home Secretary, "There I saw a chubby-cheeked little girl. She was wide awake. I have never seen a finer baby." Dark-haired, with dark blue eyes, she weighed 6 lbs. 11 ozs. at birth.

THE CECIL

(which you saw on page 24)

DEMOLISHED

Nearly 12,000 lots were listed in the catalogue of the auction sale at the Hotel Cecil, which was sold to make way for offices, early in 1930. Sixty pianos, 500,000 pieces of silver plate, 100,000 bottles of wine, 250 dining tables and the furnishings of 600 bedrooms were among the things that came under the hammer. In August, three hundred workmen walked in to begin the job of pulling down the building, working night and day so that they could be finished in seventeen weeks.

THE R101

world's biggest airship, was built at the Royal Airship Works, Cardington, and although the Air Ministry had confidently announced that she would be ready by the spring of 1928, it was not until October 1929, that she made her trial flight. In June, she flew over London during the Air Display, then went back to Cardington for alterations. In drizzling rain, on the night of October 4, she cast off from her mooring and after circling round Bedford headed for London. First stop from there was to be Egypt.

DISASTER

AT 2 A.M. NEXT MORNING —

R101, watched only by a little grey-haired Frenchman who was poaching in a wood, flew into a hillside near Beauvais, in France, and was completely destroyed by fire. "I noticed that the airship was not going steadily" said Rabouille, the poacher, "and I saw the lights go out twice. There was one loud explosion and two others and a terrific glare from the flames. It went up in the air and there was an end to it. Fini ! fini !"

46 MEN PERISHED

out of a total of 54 passengers and crew ; two more died later from their injuries. Lord Thomson, Secretary of State for Air, and Sir Sefton Brancker, Director of Civil Aviation, both were killed. On the morning before the flight, Brancker, who was never known to be nervous, seemed fidgety. Friends noticed that his manner was different, and afterwards his private letters showed that he knew all was not well with the airship.

THEIR BODIES

LYING IN STATE

in Westminster Hall, were passed by hundreds of people, who filed by in a continuous stream from 8 a.m. to midnight on October 10. The following day the coffins were taken to Cardington and, near sunset, were buried in a common grave within sight of the airship sheds.

AT THE INQUIRY

a 15-foot model of R101, about one-fiftieth the size of the airship and constructed for exhibition at the Olympia Aero Show the previous year, was suspended in the hall. Sir John Simon, chairman, and two assessors, Lt.-Col. Moore-Brabazon and Professor Inglis issued their findings the following April. Immediate cause of the disaster, said the report, was a sudden loss of gas after fabric had been torn by rough weather; sparks from a broken electric circuit had caused the fire; trials had been inadequate. No Government department, high official or group of individuals was held to be responsible.

ANOTHER AIR SMASH THAT YEAR

killed all six occupants (among them Lord Dufferin, Lady Ednam and Sir Edward Ward) of a German Junkers monoplane, piloted by Lt.-Col. George Henderson, which exploded and collapsed over Meopham, Kent, while being flown from Le Touquet to Croydon in July. It was a mysterious crash; pieces of the machine were scattered over a five miles radius (the engine, shown on the left, was found nearly a mile away from the plane), but the petrol tanks were found intact. After investigation, the Aeronautical Research Committee decided the accident was due to "air-buffeting" which broke off the tail of the plane.

BUT —

—THE CONQUEST OF THE AIR WENT ON—
408·8 miles an hour!

Flight-Lieutenant G. H. Stainforth, member of the British team that, two weeks before, raced for the Schneider Trophy and set up a new world's record of 379.05 m.p.h., attacked his own record on September 29, and surpassed all previous speeds. In an S6B seaplane, fitted with 2,600 h.p. Sprint Rolls-Royce engine, he hurtled five times over the Solent three-kilometre course, and set up a new world's record of 408.8 m.p.h. As the plane settled on the water after the flight, Stainforth, his face damp with oil and salt-sea spray, climbed out of the cockpit.

AND IN GERMANY . . .
10 Miles high!

Two scientists, Professor Piccard and his assistant, Dr. Kippur, at 4 a.m. on May 27, clambered into an airtight metal sphere hanging from a balloon and set off to explore the upper air.   For seventeen hours nothing was heard of them ; then from an Alpine hamlet came news that they had landed safely on a glacier in the Tyrol, after drifting from Germany, across Austria, to Italy ; reaching a height of 52,100 feet—nearly ten miles.   Speaking on the telephone to the "Daily Express," Piccard said : "The flight has proved that the stratosphere is navigable and that man, with modern technical methods, will be able to master the high pressure and the cold."

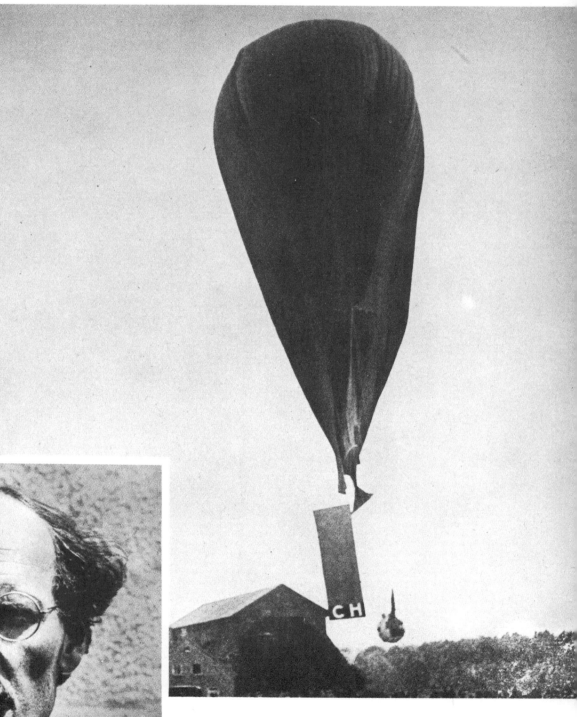

 THE PROFESSOR —

—WHEN HE LANDED 17 HOURS LATER, BROUGHT BACK THIS PICTURE

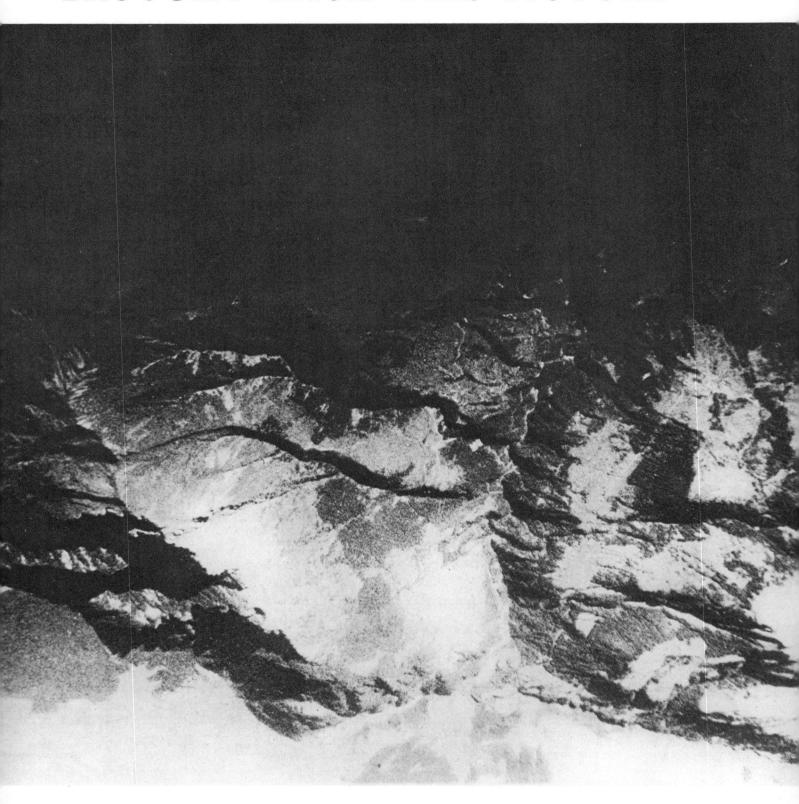

of the region around Mt. Sentis in the Swiss Alps taken from a camera in the balloon, ten miles up. Never before had any man taken such a view of the earth, showing the darkness of night and the light of day. Professor Piccard had shown how clear the air is in the stratosphere; he claimed that planes of the future would need to fly in these upper regions, where the atmosphere permits speed three times as fast as down below.

OTHER RECORDS WERE . .
Malcolm Campbell — 245·73 m.p.h.

Travelling faster than man had ever travelled on land before, he drove his 1,400 h.p. Napier-engined car "Blue Bird" up and down the sands at Daytona Beach, Florida, where Segrave had set up new records two years before. At home, Mrs. Campbell sent her message : "It is simply wonderful. I am very happy. I send you a wireless kiss across the Atlantic. But don't do it again." That was in February.

165

and on water 103·49 m.p.h. by Kaye Don

On the Parana River at Buenos Aires, in the 4,000 h.p. "Miss England II," which had been recovered from Lake Windermere (see Page 152), Kaye Don regained for Britain the world's water speed record that had been held by the American, Gar Wood. "The acceleration was like a kick in the back" he said. "The wind suddenly seemed to become solid. Spray stung the face as though it were made up of gravel chips." That was in April.

THAT YEAR "ORPS" DIED

Sir William Orpen, ordered a complete rest by his doctors in May, went on holiday to recuperate, but returned to London to work on a picture, "Palm Sunday," which was the sensation of the year's Royal Academy. He died from overwork in September, at the age of fifty-two. In little more than thirty years he had produced nearly six hundred portraits and groups. A slight, lovable Irishman, he delighted in telling anecdotes. One of his favourites concerned two Irish railway travellers who were looking from the window at the scenery. "Look, Gogarty," said one; "I would give £5 to be able to see that view just for a few minutes." Without a word, the other rose and pulled the communication cord, saying: "You shall have your wish."

Here is "Orps" with his picture "Pavlova" which was finished in March.

— PAVLOVA WHO ALSO DIED

from heart trouble, while on tour at The Hague in January, was said to be the greatest dancer of all time. At ten years of age she had gone into the Imperial School of Ballet at St. Petersburg and trained for ten years as a dancer. Then Fokine, famous ballet master, made for her "The Swan" ballet. It became the hallmark of Pavlova; she herself became known to the world as "The Swan." Famous in Europe, she first came to England with a special medal from the King of Sweden, but knowing nobody, called on a small theatrical agent to act for her. "Do you act, sing or dance?" he asked. "I dance" said Pavlova. "Dance, eh?" grunted the agent. "Well, drop in to-morrow at eleven and bring yer tights with yer."

167

AND ARNOLD BENNETT DIED

in March at the age of 63.   Novelist, critic, dramatist, he liked to regard his work as a business, not an art, and he made about £20,000 a year from his writings.   Lord Castlerosse, to whom Sir William Orpen once sent this caricature of Arnold Bennett, wrote in the "Evening Standard": "Arnold Bennett was the greatest man of our time. When the sparkle has gone out of Shaw, the realism out of Kipling . . . Arnold Bennett will still be read."

A memory of Deauville.

my dear Lordship. How did you do it? why? send him back to the five towns. Love willie

A NATIONAL CABINET

—was formed. Here are (on steps) Macdonald, Thomas, Lord Reading, Baldwin, Snowden, (and above, left to right) Samuel, Neville Chamberlain, Hoare and Lord Sankey in the garden at Downing Street. World economic systems had been shaken since the Wall Street slump of 1929. With millions of people in want (there were 30,000,000 industrial workers alone unemployed all over the world), stocks of coffee were being destroyed in Brazil, rubber was being burned in Malay, food, clothing, luxuries, all were being over-produced for prices that would not cover cost of production. War debts and reparations were helping to bankrupt poorer countries and foreign depositors in the Bank of England began to draw out their money. At end of July the Government's Economy Committee reported that £120,000,000 would have to be found to balance the Budget. Cuts in unemployment benefits were proposed—and on this, Labour split. Arthur Henderson, then Foreign Secretary, with most of the party behind him, led the Opposition against MacDonald, Snowden and Thomas. There was deadlock, and at this stage King George V intervened. He suggested a National Government formed from the various parties.

AT THE ELECTION —

— Britain's Oldest Voter

was Mrs. Merriott, who at 106, was helped to the polling booth at North Croydon.

Fourteen million people voted for a National Government; seven million voted for keeping a Labour Government. MacDonald was again Prime Minister; and the new Cabinet contained four Labour representatives, four Conservatives and two Liberals. Stanley Baldwin was Lord President of the Council, Neville Chamberlain Chancellor of the Exchequer.

ALL FRIENDS TOGETHER

to keep us on the Gold Standard. But not even MacDonald, Baldwin and Thomas (left to right, Thomas is giving MacDonald some white heather for good luck), could control the drain on the Bank of England. Even £130,000,000 borrowed from America and France had become exhausted. Britain had not enough gold to back up its banknotes, and on September 20, we came off the Gold Standard. The pound slumped to thirteen shillings, but cheapening the price of goods to buyers abroad sent up exports, and brought down unemployment figures. British bankers' policy of granting huge loans for foreign investment had partly brought on this financial crisis: when Austrian, German and Central European banks collapsed, British investors were unable to get their money back.

ECONOMY LED TO

stoppage of work in December on the £5,000,000 Cunard liner "534," now the "Queen Mary." Designed as the finest, fastest and safest ship ever built, she was to have been launched three months later, to make her maiden voyage in 1933. Banks, however, refused to finance construction; notices were posted up in the shipyard at Clydebank, Glasgow, and 5,000 skilled men suddenly found themselves unemployed.

AND —

Invergordon

Sir Austen Chamberlain was First Lord of the Admiralty when, in September, Atlantic Fleet exercises were cancelled owing to unrest among the sailors because of pay cuts. Administrative blundering had brought about this mutiny; sailors had not been told of the cuts or the need for them and first news came when some of them went ashore to buy evening newspapers. For two tense days, the Fleet lay at anchor at Invergordon, men carrying out all ordinary duties but refusing to put to sea. Then the ships were ordered to their various home stations and shortly after, certain cuts were adjusted.

LONDON FLOOD-LIT

Ten thousand floodlights turned London into the world's brightest city in September, to honour Michael Faraday who, one hundred years before, had discovered the principles of electrical magnetism which are needed in nearly all our modern applications of electricity. In the greatest revel since Armistice night, crowds jammed in parks and streets to see the sights of London by night.

BIG BEN 👉

Battersea Power Station

—AND HENRY VII's CHAPEL at Westminster Abbey

Two hundred delegates from twenty foreign countries came to floodlit London for the International Illumination Congress. Then they toured Britain: all over the country, cathedrals, churches, memorials and public buildings stood at night in the beams from floodlights. Each evening, half a million people flocked to London's central area; bus routes ceased to exist, police control broke down and everybody just kept shuffling along.

EXILED QUEEN SAYS GOOD-BYE

With the words : "Adios Madrid ! Adios Espana !" tears running down her face, Queen Ena left Spain on April 15, travelling secretly to meet her husband, King Alfonso, who had abdicated following the news of sweeping Republican success in the municipal elections. "I know my duty" said Alfonso. "Spain does not want me, yet I have always had her welfare at heart and never have I done anything that might injure the best interests of my country. I must accept things as they are." Queen Ena signed autographs for her ladies-in-waiting (below) and met her husband in Paris the next night.

JAPANESE INVADE MANCHURIA

Japan had been given a lease on the South Manchurian Railway in 1905 ; they were to control the line and develop the railway zone.   But in 1928, there was trouble.   As a train carrying Chang Tso-Lin, Chinese ruler in Manchuria, passed over a bridge guarded by Japanese soldiers, a bomb exploded beneath it.   Tso-Lin, who had quarrelled with Japan's General Staff, was killed. On September 18, 1931, another bomb exploded beneath a train, this time killing a Japanese military officer.   It was the signal for Japan to invade Manchuria.   Chang Hsueh-Ling, Tso-Lin's son, led the Chinese armies, but within a year they were defeated and Japan was in control.   Nothing came of League of Nations protests against this invasion.

BRÜNING BECAME GERMAN DICTATOR

Germany had to take orders from the spectacled chancellor, Dr. Heinrich Brüning, in December, when his emergency decrees were accepted and signed by President von Hindenburg. Lower salaries; higher taxes; no public political meetings; political uniforms and party badges banned from the streets, these were among Brüning's measures to save another collapse of the mark and to keep Germany's internal affairs quiet. Foreign policy was taking up much of his attention. He wanted an Austro-German customs union and a satisfactory settlement of the war debts problems.

While Hitler—

1931

—for a moment despaired

He was detested by Brüning, who had said, when bringing in the emergency decrees: "The Government will flinch at nothing in defending the State against any attempt of the National Socialists to usurp power by illegal force." Here, talking to Hitler after the decrees had come into force, is his right-hand man, Goering, not yet in one of his since-famous uniforms.

"POSEIDON" SUNK

It was too late to change course after the look-out man on the 1,753-tons Chinese steamer "Yuta" first saw the British submarine "Poseidon" coming up to the surface towards the ship on June 9. Metal plates crashed ; "Poseidon," carrying out exercises in the China Sea, sank in just two minutes. In that time, thirty-one men managed to clamber through the narrow hatch to safety. Twenty-four were left trapped in the submarine ; six of them grouped in the bows. Petty Officer Willis took charge of this group, helped them fit on the new Davis escape apparatus, waited till, 3½ hours after the crash, they had all managed to squeeze out of their nearly water-filled compartment. Then he got clear himself. But eighteen men behind water-tight doors in other parts of the submarine were never seen again. Twenty in all died from the sinking of the "Poseidon." Here are four of the survivors : (left to right) Holt, Petty Officer Willis, Nagle, Clarke.

NEXT YEAR ANOTHER SUBMARINE SANK

First underwater plane carrier

M2, carrying a Parnall "Peto" seaplane (which catapulted off a runway to take off, was hoisted into hangar on deck of submarine when landing) dived into West Bay, near Dorset, on the morning of January 26. Nothing more was seen of her until after eight days' search by submarines and destroyers she was located in the sea mud. Sixty officers and men had died but nobody ever found out the cause of the disaster. Salvage work went on for months; the submarine was raised eighteen feet at the end of September, but then sank again; and soon after the M2 was abandoned.

LINDBERGH BABY KIDNAPPED

Charles Lindbergh junior, baby son of Col. and Mrs. Charles A. Lindbergh (see pages 103-5), was kidnapped at dead of night from his nursery in March. A note in his cot demanded £10,000 ransom.

A few days later, Lindbergh accepted the offer of Dr. "Jafsie" Gordon, a schoolmaster, to act as intermediary between parents and kidnappers. On April 2, "Jafsie" handed £10,000 over to a man who showed him the baby's sleeping suit, but though the ransom was paid, the baby was not returned. Then, a little more than two months later, Orville Wilson and a Negro truck driver, William Allen (below) found the baby's body, covered with dead leaves and debris, lying about four miles from the Lindbergh's home. The skull was fractured, and the coroner termed it "cold, deliberate murder."

Clues, suspects, marked ransom notes were followed up during 1932, 1933 and into 1934. In September that year, ransom money was traced to the home of a German carpenter, Bruno Hauptmann. See page 208.

AND FOUND —

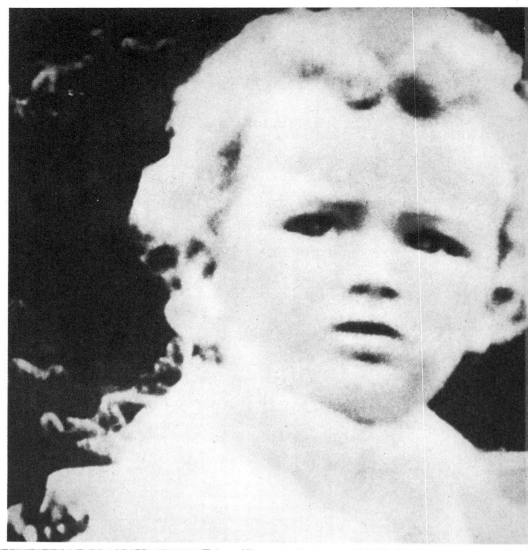

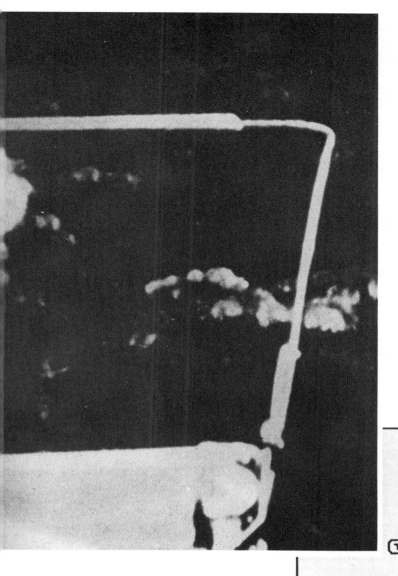

People came from miles around—

to the scene of the kidnapping. Lindbergh was looked upon as America's "Prince of Wales." Newspapers filled their front pages with stories of the crime. Each move of Lindbergh, his wife, the police, everybody, in fact, connected with the case was recorded for millions of readers. Photographs below show a postcard sent to Lindbergh. (Note spelling error in his name.)

—MURDERED

Eighty-thousand pounds were spent in the search for the kidnapper and murderer. Police had studied the kidnapper's messages, deduced that the writer was Teutonic. He spelled phonetically, used "gute" for "good." From a drawing on one of the notes they reckoned he might be a mechanic, and from emery dust found on marked ransom notes that he might be a carpenter or machinist who ground his own tools. Vague descriptions from various witnesses finally formed a picture of the suspected man. They said he weighed about 11st. 6 lbs., had a sharp nose, flat cheeks, small mouth and pointed chin.

THIS SIDE OF CARD IS FOR ADDRESS

CHAS. LINBERG
PRINCETON
N. G

BABY SAFE

INSTRUCTIONS
LATER

ACT ACCORDINGLY

ANOTHER CRIME—
FRENCH PRESIDENT ASSASSINATED

"The world's full of banditry. But I'm not a bandit. I'm a poet—I'm an idealist." So said tall, lean, 37-year-old Paul Gourgouloff, mad Russian, after firing four shots at M. Doumer, French President, on May 6, causing fatal injuries. The president had just arrived at an ex-service men's exhibition in Paris, when Gourgouloff, wearing dark glasses, pushed his way through the crowd and fired. Here he is, in police custody, after being rescued from onlookers who tried to lynch him.

2 SOLO ATLANTIC FLIGHTS

When James Allan Mollison, 27-year-old Scot, landed at New Brunswick in his tiny Puss Moth monoplane, "Heart's Content," on August 19, thirty hours after leaving Ireland, he set up three new records: First solo Atlantic flight, east to west; first Atlantic crossing by light airplane in either direction; fastest crossing from east to west. Besides these, he held the Australia-England and England-Cape flying records. He intended to fly back from America, but fog held him up and eventually he returned by steamer.

Amelia Earhart, too (see pages 113, 114), made her solo Atlantic flight in May, landing at Londonderry 14 hours 56 minutes after leaving Harbour Grace, Newfoundland.

"AMY" & "JIM" MARRIED

"My wife has been a source of inspiration to me all through the flight" said Jim Mollison after his Atlantic trip. His wife was the Amy Johnson who had made a lone flight from Australia in 1930 (see page 141). They were married ten days before the Atlantic attempt, at St. George's, Hanover Sq., London. Amy was in black, without a bouquet; her parents arrived too late for the ceremony; the best man arrived early but, at first, was barred at the church door until he had proved his identity. When it was all over, Mrs. Mollison said: "We have firmly agreed that neither of us is going to interfere with the other's flying plans."

2 CONFERENCES——one to "end" armaments

one to increase Empire trade

R. B. Bennett, then Prime Minister of Canada, fixed Ottawa, three thousand miles from Whitehall, as meeting place for an imperial conference after the 1930 conference in London turned out badly. Empire delegates met there in August to arrange trade agreements which, said critics, though they did not go far enough, were the best made up till that time.

This, the biggest of all disarmament conferences, opened in April at Geneva. Delegates were agreed on principles; they all wanted peace, they all wanted safety. But on the details of how this was to be done, the conference broke down. . .

THE HUNGER MARCHERS

Two thousand men and women walked from Scotland, South Wales, the north of England and towns on the south and east coasts in October, led by members of the National Unemployed Workers' Movement, a Communist body. Britain at this time had nearly $2\frac{3}{4}$ millions unemployed and they were feeling the effects of economy measures that had brought the fall of the Labour Government a year before (see page 169). Bitter criticism was being made against the "means test" law which gave local authorities power to investigate the whole household income before granting relief to any unemployed person in a family. Converging on London, the "hunger marchers" met in Hyde Park (below), and around Nelson's monument in Trafalgar Square for public demonstrations. Agitators caused riots at many of the meetings, bringing clashes with the police (above).

1932

THAT NIGHT—

1932

— they marched to the Commons

with a petition carrying a million signatures protesting against the means test. Thousands of onlookers gathered at Westminster, Whitehall, and Charing Cross. Traffic was dislocated, fireworks were thrown into the crowds. A man with an iron bar tried to hit a mounted police officer and was dragged away by five policemen (above). Parked motor cars were overturned, windows were broken, fifteen people were injured.

and next morning

railings around Hyde Park were found lying on the pavement after having been torn up by hooligans. The hunger marchers cost London £230 a day for maintenance during their stay; many of the genuine unemployed among them went home by rail at a special rate of three miles a penny.

FACES IN THE NEWS

PREMIER

of Austria was 4 ft. 11 ins. Dr. Dollfuss, simple, modest, outright Catholic, who the following year took over dictatorship powers and ruled by decrees. Jokes about his size became famous. It was said that he broke his leg one day, falling off a ladder; he had been picking a dandelion. But tragedy was waiting for Dollfuss (see page 211).

PRESIDENT-ELECT

of America early in 1932, was Franklin Delano Roosevelt, then governor of New York State. Hoover, the president, was seeking re-election, but in November Roosevelt polled 25½ million votes to Hoover's 16 millions.

PRESIDENT

of Irish Free State was De Valera, who displaced Cosgrave in February. Born in America, of a Spanish father, Irish mother, he had come to Ireland at the age of two. Revolutionary, intense nationalist, his intention was to break away from Britain (see pages 25, 34-36).

PRESIDENT

of Germany was 85-year-old field-marshal Hindenburg (see page 81) here seen being kissed by his grand-daughter on his birthday. It was suggested at this time that Hindenburg was not in full possession of his faculties, and that after a little exertion he became absentminded.

1st CHANCELLOR

of Germany after the dismissal of Brüning (see page 177) in May, was Von Papen, suave, quick-witted officer who got virtual cancellation of Germany's war reparations at a Lausanne conference in July. But Papen was unpopular with the German people, and after the November elections Hindenburg dismissed him.

2nd CHANCELLOR

after Brüning, was Kurt von Schleicher, formerly in the German Defence Ministry. He had the army behind him, Von Papen and Hitler against him, and the following January after Papen had presented a Nazi-Nationalist plan of government to Hindenburg, Schleicher was dismissed to make way for Hitler.

STARVED

Gandhi, back in India, after a fruitless Round Table Conference (see page 148), began to starve himself to death in September, as protest against certain Indian government electoral measures. After six days it was agreed these measures would be amended.

KILLED HIMSELF

Kreuger, Swedish match king, controlling 250 match factories in 43 countries, shot himself in a Paris Hotel on March 12. His liabilities totalled more than £58,000,000, his assets under £5,000,000.

RESIGNED

Snowden, lord privy seal in the National government (see page 169) was bitterly opposed to all trade tariffs and resigned after the Ottawa agreements had been made (see page 184). Sir Herbert Samuel, National Liberal leader, who also opposed tariffs, resigned with Snowden.

TOM WALLS WINS DERBY

When the 100-6 winner of the 1932 Derby passed the post, superstitious racegoers noted that horse, owner and jockey each had thirteen letters in their names. April the Fifth, owned by Tom Kirby Walls and ridden by Frederick Lane, pushed up past Orwell, the 5-4 favourite and galloped on to finish threequarters of a length in front of Prince Aga Khan's Dastur. Orwell, with at least £200,000 laid on him, came in ninth.

3 MEN SPLIT THE ATOM

Experimenting at the Cavendish Laboratory, Cambridge, two young British scientists, Dr. Cockroft and Dr. Walton (shown here) working under Professor Lord Rutherford, bombarded and split the atom in May. They used electric power of between 120,000 to 600,000 volts, sending millions of particles through a vacuum tube at speeds of 6,000 miles a second. Prophecies that the world would blow up when the atom was split were wrong. "Although the discovery is of immense scientific importance" said Dr. Cockroft, "it is not of immediate practical value." Doctor Walton, in this picture, is adjusting one of the vacuums in the atom-splitting apparatus. When the power is switched on, lightning flashes crackle in the gap between the two metal spheres behind him.

DARTMOOR RIOTS, PRISON BLAZE

Three hundred convicts in Dartmoor prison mutinied on Sunday, January 24, and for a time, got complete control. They set fire to buildings, burned most of the prison records, raided the prison officers' canteen, drank all the liquor and scattered the cigarettes around. Troops in Plymouth, who were summoned from church parade, turned out in full war equipment and waited in Army lorries with machine guns, ready to drive to the prison. Warders and police, however, managed to regain control after fighting in which eighty-four convicts were shot or injured by batons. Inscription over the gate at Dartmoor prison means: "Spare the vanquished."

THE CONVICTS

— MUTINIED

Trouble had simmered for many weeks, partly because of prison diet complaints, partly because many men had been drafted to other prisons, leaving at Dartmoor the worst kind of criminal offenders. When breakfast was served in the cells that Sunday morning, spoons rattled against bars, plates were flung at warders. There was no sugar in the porridge, cried the convicts and the demand grew louder: "We want the governor." Time came for the men to march to chapel for morning service; they filed out of their cells, then suddenly broke ranks and rioted.

Embers in the fireplace of the prison governor's office were used by convicts to start the blaze which destroyed the central block of buildings (above). No prison officers were seriously hurt, though a few (including this warder) received minor injuries. Thirty men were tried after the mutiny, sentences given them ranging from 22 years penal servitude downward. There was public agitation for the prison to be closed, as it was unfit for modern conditions, having been built in 1806 for French and American prisoners of war.

HE HELPED WARDERS

O'Donovan, a Brighton man serving life sentence for murder, went to the help of the prison governor, who at first had been attacked in mistake for a steward. For this, O'Donovan had five years taken off his sentence. All roads round Dartmoor were watched after the mutiny and motorists were held up, their papers examined (below). No prisoners escaped during the outbreak.

ANOTHER CONFERENCE

Sixty-six nations sent 168 representatives to the World Economic Conference which opened at the new Geological Museum, South Kensington on June 12. They hoped to find means of ending world trade depression, but the conference broke up at the end of the following month with practically nothing accomplished. Here is King George V speaking at the beginning of the conference. Next to him is Sir Eric Drummond, then outgoing Secretary-General of the League of Nations and on extreme right of picture, horn-rimmed M. Avenol who was shortly to be the new Secretary-General. Ramsay MacDonald presided over this conference. Sir John Simon, proposed as one of Britain's delegates, fell ill before the opening date and his place was taken by Anthony Eden, then Parliamentary Under-Secretary for Foreign Affairs. Here he is with Arthur Henderson, who had been president of the disarmament conference (see page 184).

THE HEADQUARTERS OF THE "DAILY EXPRESS."

◆

THE BATTLE OF THE NEWSPAPERS
2,000,000 — 2,000,000

The "Daily Express," after a circulation battle which has lasted months, has announced a net sale exceeding

2,000,000 copies a day.

It is the first daily newspaper in the world to be able to do so.

The circulation battle has been won by the "Daily Express." It is the first newspaper to add to its net sale the readers necessary to pass the 2,000,000 mark.

By LORD BEAVERBROOK. 1933

The "Daily Express" is, of course, more widely read by the shopkeepers than any other newspaper.

A discussion between the shopkeepers and me is therefore both natural and desirable.

I hold the view that shopkeepers should replenish their stocks now, and I have no hesitation in saying so.

I believe that prices must rise. I mean both wholesale prices and retail prices. I believe the rise is taking place now and here.

The fact is that the value of money has fallen much more rapidly than the price of merchandise has increased.

There is already a considerable leeway to be made up between the fall in money and the limited rise that has taken place in goods.

It is said that money— I refer to pounds and dollars—may be stabilised. I think stabilisation is a long way off.

But even if stabilisation takes place there must be a rise in prices. And if there is no stabilisation there must be a still greater rise in prices.

M.P.s CALL FOR POLICE INQUIRY

DAILY EXPRESS 2,000,000

Extract from the front page on July 1, 1933

193

1933

FLIGHT OVER
EVEREST

35,000 FEET UP

Everest, highest mountain in the world, 29,141 ft. high, was flown over on April 3 by four men—the Marquis of Clydesdale, Lt.-Col. Blacker, Flgt. Lt. McIntyre and S. R. Bonnett—in two airplanes of the £19,000 Mount Everest expedition financed by Lady Houston. They cleared the summit only by 100 feet, owing to the terrific down-draught. For fifteen minutes they circled Everest then then had to return as McIntyre's camera-man, Bonnett, who had accidentally trodden on an oxygen feed-pipe and bound the break with a handkerchief, collapsed in his cockpit. After this flight, orders came to return home to England and further flights were forbidden. On April 20, however, without a word to anybody at the base camp, the pilots set off again, Bonnett's place taken by cameraman A. L. Fisher. The two planes, rising to 35,000 feet, brought back infra-red long-range pictures of the Himalayas (above) as well as close-ups of Everest, and the second flight was a greater success than the first. Oxygen suits (right), worn by the flyers were made in London and tested by apparatus which repro-duced atmospheric conditions at 40,000 feet, 60°C. below zero. Welcomed back in England, the pilots received presentations and the picture shows Lord Clydesdale (left) being congratulated by the Master of Sempill.

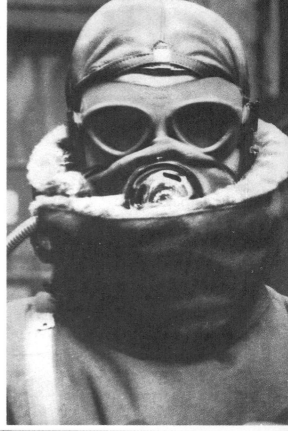

LARGEST AIRSHIP CRASHES

Only three were saved in America's worst air disaster which came shortly after midnight on April 4 when the £1,000,000 U.S. naval airship Akron, with 77 officers and men aboard, crashed into the sea off the coast of New Jersey after being caught in a thunderstorm. During rescue work, a semi-dirigible airship J4 also crashed, killing two of her crew. Tangled girders of the Akron were hauled from the sea by U.S. minesweeper Falcon the following month (right). Akron, world's largest airship when launched and eight feet longer than Britain's R101 (see page 157), is shown in the picture above, flying over New York city.

£2,250,000 FIRE

L'Atlantique, 42,500-ton luxury liner, insured mostly with British underwriters for £2¼ millions, caught fire near the Channel Islands when on her way to Le Havre for dry-docking and repairs. The rapidly spreading fire got out of control and orders were given for the crew of 230 to abandon ship. Nineteen men were drowned or burned to death. L'Atlantique, built at a cost of £3,000,000 only eighteen months before was the largest and finest ship, after the Ile de France, in the French merchant marine. For nearly two days she drifted in the Channel and a French torpedo-boat destroyer hovered nearby, ready to blow her up if she became a menace to coastal shipping. Seamen from tugs standing by managed to get lines aboard to tow her into dock at Cherbourg Harbour (below). Still hanging at the side of the burned out hull was a lifeboat (above), its tackle fouled. Defects in L'Atlantique's electric wiring were reported to have caused the fire.

197

FRONT PAGE MEN

BACK FROM MOSCOW

Thousands of people at London's Liverpool Street station on July 5, welcomed home two British engineers, Leslie Thornton and William MacDonald, who had been released from prison in Moscow. On the night of March 11, the Metropolitan-Vickers' office in Moscow was raided by secret police and six British employees were arrested on charges of bribery, spying and machine-wrecking. After six days' trial, two men were set free, two were deported and Thornton and MacDonald put in prison. Britain made protests, put an embargo on Russian imports and secured the release of the two engineers.

FIRE-RAISING CASE

Leopold Harris (right), leader of a gang of fire-raisers who had cost insurance firms nearly three million pounds paid out for fraudulent claims, went to prison for fourteen years after a two-year investigation by William Crocker, London solicitor, had brought about the arrest of sixteen men. Captain Miles (left), then chief officer of London's Salvage Corps, was found guilty on five charges of conspiracy and corruption. He got four years' penal servitude.

"KICKED UPSTAIRS"

Bearded Italo Balbo, picturesque, arrogant head of Italy's air force, organised a mass formation flight of twenty-four seaplanes from Rome to Chicago and back in July. So popular was he on his return from this 11,800 miles flight that Mussolini was pleased to appoint him governor of Libya in November; taking Balbo out of the limelight and putting him in virtual exile.

THE LOCH NESS MONSTER

Tourists with field-glasses and telescopes came from all over the country in the summer of 1933, to look for a monster that was said to be swimming in the waters of Loch Ness. Hotels at Inverness filled up with visitors drawn to the best holiday attraction in the Scottish Highlands. Regularly every week came stories that the monster had been seen. Photographs like the one above were taken to prove the existence of a creature which had, said witnesses, two or three humps. Seaside artists gave their impressions of the Loch Ness Monster in the sand (below); it was a music-hall joke, a "silly-season" topic. Bertram Mills offered £20,000 to anybody who could capture it alive and deliver it to his circus—but nobody got the £20,000.

199

THE GENERAL RAN AWAY . .

General Tang Yu-Lin, Chinese governor of Jehol province, was looked on as the "Chinese Napoleon"; he was the hope of all China in the war against Japanese troops invading Manchuria (see page 176); but on March 4 he was found to be using military trucks to move his personal property, leaving soldiers without ammunition or guns. As the Japanese troops came nearer, making rapid marches across snow-covered ground (below), Tang Yu-Lin was missing. He had been seen riding swiftly away from Jehol city towards the boundary of the province. His flight helped Japan quickly to get control over the whole of Jehol and set up the "independent" state of Manchukuo.

INCOMER & OUTGOER

Though Democrat Roosevelt (right) had beaten Republican Hoover (left) in the 1932 presidential elections (see page 187), American laws demanded that the change-over should not take place for four months. In that interval, America was at the bottom of trade depression. Hundreds of banks were shut, prices were at their lowest and the nation faced a budget deficit for the financial year, estimated at more than £400,000,000. On March 4, Roosevelt became president and immediately asked for powers to intervene in private business with State enterprises. He got them and brought in measures to help industry, business, finance, the fifteen million unemployed without State relief and the thirty million farmers burdened with mortgages they could not pay. This was Roosevelt's "New Deal" for the American people.

ATTEMPT ON ROOSEVELT'S LIFE

A sallow-looking man in a brown suit stepped out of the crowd welcoming Roosevelt to Miami, Florida, in February and fired five shots which missed Roosevelt but hit his companions. Most seriously hit was Anton Cermak, who had followed "Big Bill" Thompson (see page 102), as mayor of Chicago. The would-be assassin was Joseph Zangara, Italian anarchist, who said when taken by the police: "I want to kill the President. If I had a machine gun in my hands I would kill all the presidents and all the kings, and then burn all the money in a bonfire."

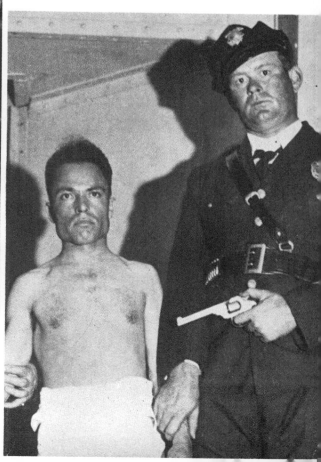

BUT ANOTHER MAN DIED

Nobody knew that Cermak was badly hurt as he was led away to an ambulance (above) but in hospital nineteen days later, he died. Zangara was sentenced to death for murder. In March, he went to the electric chair. "Go ahead, press the button," he said, and died laughing.

201

REPEAL OF PROHIBITION

Though alcoholic drinks had been prohibited in the United States since 1919, Americans had never really co-operated with the government in this matter and evasion of the Prohibition laws was a national sport. But contempt for this side of the law had encouraged contempt for the rest of the law. "Bootleggers" (sellers of illegal drink) were followed by gangsters and racketeers. Murder, violence, daylight robbery had become commonplace and because of this one of Roosevelt's early moves was to bring in a Bill that licensed the sale of liquor.

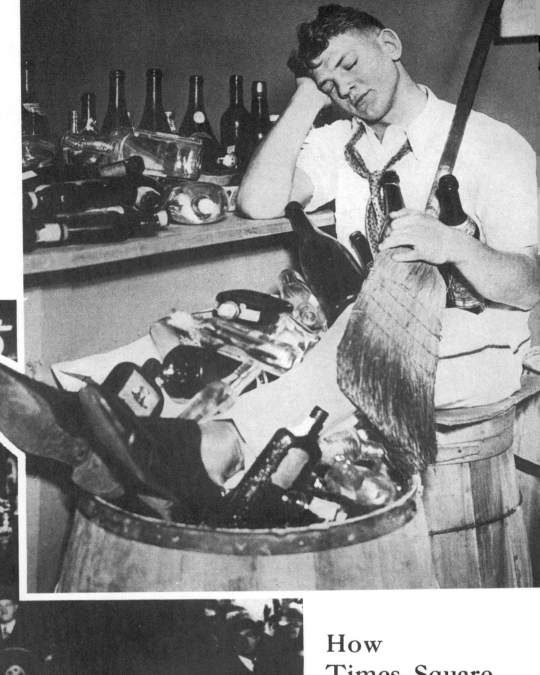

How Times Square Welcomed it

New York went "repeal-mad" on December 5 when, for the first time in nearly 14 years, beer, wine and spirit drinking became legal. Broadway and Times Square (left) were packed with people watching the electric news signs; traffic was blocked and nine hundred police were powerless to clear a way. Bar-tenders and waiters in all drinking places were kept rushing about dealing with customers' orders, and next-morning's hang-over (here's a sample of it), was shared by millions of exuberant Americans of the night before.

HITLER BECOMES CHANCELLOR

As leader of the largest political party (representing 13¾ million votes), Hitler had been received by Hindenburg in the previous July, accompanied by Von Papen (see page 187). Hitler, as though he were addressing a crowd and not the president, demanded the chancellorship on his own terms, giving him dictatorial powers. Hindenburg, contemptuous; said to Papen: "Let Hitler mend his manners or I will appoint him to be a village postmaster." Papen became chancellor, then Schleicher (see page 187), but by January, Nazi influence had reached the point where not even Hindenburg could ignore Hitler. Papen, who had joined forces with Hitler, saw the president. Schleicher was dismissed, Hitler was made chancellor, and in March Nazis polled 17¼ million votes at the elections. Here is Hitler looking down on the crowds as they cheered him after the election results were known.

AND—

Hitler's passionate desire was to create 100% Germany for 100% Germans, and as soon as he came to power Nazis started a purge of all "non-German" elements. Internationalists, pacifists, the Church, all were attacked, but most bitter of all was the Nazis war on Jews. Notices carried by pickets outside Jewish-owned stores, read : "Germans ! Be on your guard ! Don't buy from Jews !" Stocky shaven-headed Julius Streicher, chief Nazi Jew-baiter and one of Hitler's oldest supporters, organised the boycott.

FIVE MEN WERE ACCUSED

of burning the Reichstag, Germany's Houses of Parliament, on the night of February 27, a few days before the elections. "A communist plot !" cried Hitler and Goering, as soon as they got to the fire. Near the burning ruins, police arrested a half-wit Dutch Communist, Van de Lubbe (shown left, in court with head hung), whom records showed to be a fire-raiser. Later, three Bulgarian Communists in Germany, Dimitrov, Popov and Tanev, with the chairman of the Reichstag Communists, Ernst Torgler, were also arrested. Nazis, working up a Communist scare reminiscent of Britain's 'Zinoviev letter' outcry (see page 64), went back into power after the elections with a record majority and passed a Bill giving Hitler dictator's powers. In September, the five men accused

OF SETTING THE—

REICHSTAG ON FIRE

were brought to trial; Van de Lubbe pleaded guilty and was sentenced to death. Dimitrov, hero of the trial because of his courage and pointed remarks (when a witness could not be found, he asked if the concentration camps had been searched), was acquitted with Popov and Tanev; Torgler was acquitted but kept in 'protective custody.' Evidence during the 57-day trial showed that the fire, which started in thirty different parts of the building, was blazing fiercely only two minutes five seconds after Van de Lubbe, a shambling, half-blind creature, had gone in. He had only household fire-lighters but experts testified that large amounts of petrol and chemicals had started the fire. If Van de Lubbe had accomplices, how did they escape? Anti-Nazis claimed that it was not the Communists but the Nazis themselves who set the Reichstag on fire.

PRINCESS MARINA BECAME—

engaged to King George V's youngest son, Prince George (now Duke of Kent), while he was holiday-making in Greece. Grand-daughter of King George of Greece, who was brother of Queen Alexandra (see page 80), Princess Marina came to England in September; during the next few months, most popular hats sold were copies of hats worn by the princess. Two favourites were a drooping brimmed hat, with high crown and pompon on top, and the perky pill-box with little upstanding feather at the side which she wears in this picture.

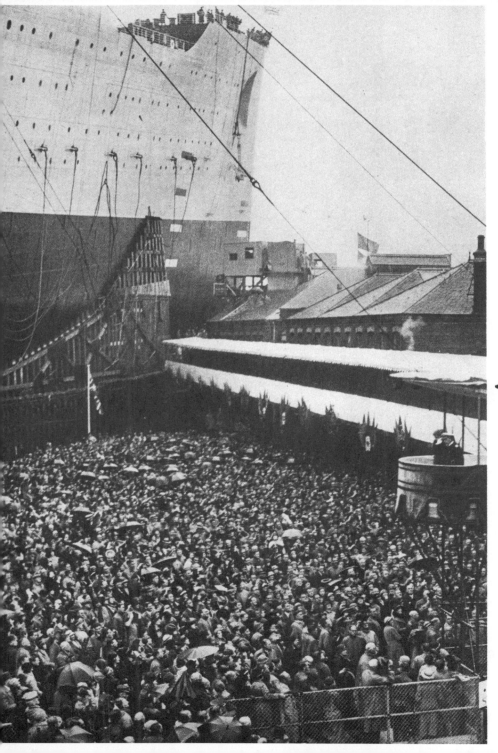

DUCHESS OF KENT

was the title of Princess Marina after her marriage in Westminster Abbey on November 29. Prince George had been made Duke of Kent in October. After the ceremony, the bride and bridegroom returned to Buckingham Palace for a Greek wedding service and then came out on the balcony to acknowledge cheers (above). This group, left to right, is : Lady Mary Cambridge, Princess Elizabeth, Princess Nicholas of Greece, King George V, Princess Margaret Rose, Duchess of Kent, Prince Nicholas of Greece, Duke of Kent, Queen Mary.

ANOTHER ROYAL OCCASION

In pouring rain, 250,000 people gathered at Clydebank, Scotland, in September, to see Queen Mary christen and launch what was the world's largest liner (see page 171). "I am glad to name this ship "Queen Mary" she said. King George V was there. He said: "As a sailor I have deep pleasure in coming to watch the launching by the Queen of this grand and beautiful ship." Smoothly, the ship moved down the slipway and slid into the Clyde.

CRIME: IN AMERICA

PUBLIC ENEMY No. 1

John Dillinger, American gangster who had killed fourteen men and got nearly £70,000 from hold-up robberies, was ambushed and killed outside a Chicago cinema by sixteen detectives after his woman friend had betrayed him to the police. As he came out from seeing a gangster film "Manhattan Melodrama" nineteen bullets entered his head and body. They ended the £20,000 hunt for America's "Public Enemy No. 1."

FORMER MILLIONAIRE BANKER

Joseph W. Harriman, 67-year-old American banker, was given a 4½-years' sentence in June for misapplying his bank's funds and making false entries. Here he is with his wife after the trial. As he passed through the prison gates in July, he said to reporters: "I will come back." "In banking?" they asked. "In anything . . ." said Harriman ". . . Peanuts, bananas—there's always opportunity."

LINDBERGH BABY'S MURDERER

Bruno Hauptmann (see page 180), found in September after an £80,000 search, sat unmoved during his trial at Flemington, New Jersey. Treated as America's biggest show, it dragged on till February 1935, when Hauptmann was found guilty and sentenced to death. Making two unsuccessful appeals, he finally went to the electric chair on April 4, 1936, more than four years after the time of the kidnapping.

THEY GOT HIM AT LAST

Al Capone, a fat little man with thick lips and a scar running from chin to left ear, was moved from a penitentiary to Alcatraz prison (America's "Devil's Island"), in August. For six years Capone had been America's greatest gangster. Seven times he had been brought to trial, but juries were afraid to convict him until 1931, when he had been given an eleven-year sentence for tax evasion.

IN FRANCE: THE STAVISKY CASE

Serge Stavisky (below), a Russian Jew, worked his way up through the French underworld till he was a very successful swindler. (His wife, whose picture is on the right, was cleared of complicity.) Politicians, police, scores of minor officials were in his pay, which explains why his fraudulent schemes were so long undisclosed. He had been arrested in 1926 on complaint of two brokers who said he had swindled them out of £70,000. But Stavisky was "provisionally" released, his trial postponed nineteen times and the Paris police handled the case forty-five times without troubling to re-arrest him. In 1933, however, he issued fraudulent bonds in the name of the municipal pawnshop of Bayonne (pawnshops are State-controlled in France), and Dalimier, minister of the government at that time, signed a letter recommending these bonds. The truth got out and Stavisky, with a false passport given him by the police, fled from Paris. He was found shot on January 8, at Chamonix near the Swiss border. Suicide was the official verdict, but many French people believed he had been murdered to keep him quiet. France rocked with the scandal, the government fell, politicians were denounced, and on February 6, because of Stavisky exposures, thirty thousand people rioted in Paris. Seventeen were killed and many thousands injured.

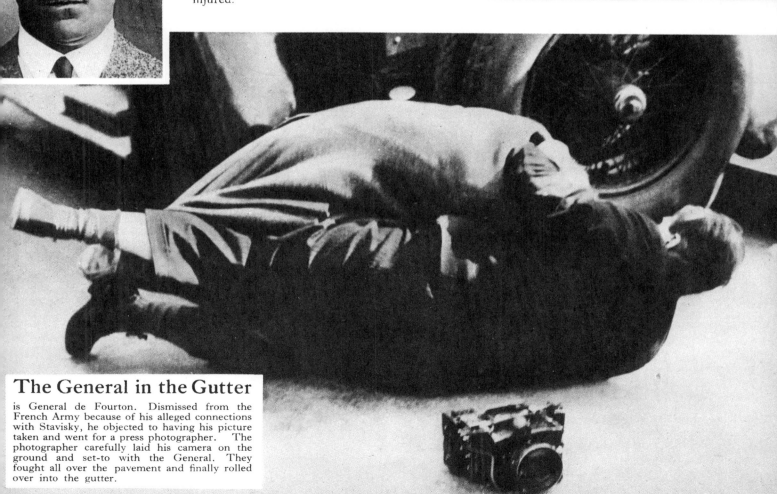

The General in the Gutter

is General de Fourton. Dismissed from the French Army because of his alleged connections with Stavisky, he objected to having his picture taken and went for a press photographer. The photographer carefully laid his camera on the ground and set-to with the General. They fought all over the pavement and finally rolled over into the gutter.

and, also in France POLITICAL CRIME

War nearly came to Europe in October with the assassination of King Alexander of Jugoslavia at Marseilles, while on a State visit to France to discuss plans for more settled relations in Europe. Louis Barthou, French Foreign Minister, was also killed. Here are the two men riding in the car as it left the quayside at Marseilles; a few minutes later, King Alexander was dead, Barthou dying.

POLICE RUSHED

towards a man who broke away from the crowd at the roadside and jumped on the running board of the royal car. They were too late. The man had thrust his arm through the window and fired several shots before a mounted escort struck him down (left). One bullet pierced the king's lung, another smashed his shoulder and a bullet also smashed the arm of 72-year-old Louis Barthou, causing his death nearly two hours later.

THE ASSASSIN

Vlada Georgiev, a Balkan terrorist who had on him a false passport in the name of Petrus Kalemen, was torn and trampled by the mob, and died the same day. Fanatic and revolutionary, he had been working for years on a plan to blow up the League of Nations building at Geneva. He had meant to do that after killing King Alexander.

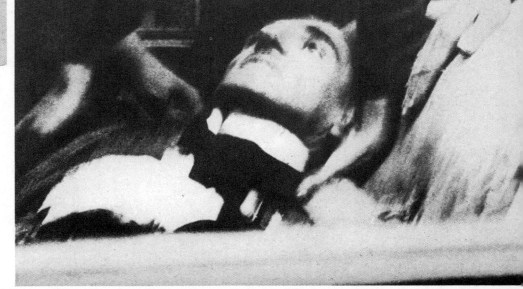

DOLLFUSS MURDERED BY NAZIS

On July 21, a Berlin picture news-agency sent out photographs of Dr. Anton Rintelen (Austrian minister in Rome and friend of the Nazis), with the caption: "New Austrian Chancellor—Hold for Release." Four days later, while Chancellor Dollfuss (see page 187) was holding a Cabinet meeting in Vienna's "No. 10 Downing Street," news came to him that there had been an uprising of Austrian Nazis and some of them were on their way to kill him. In another part of the city, fourteen men had seized the broadcasting studios and sent out the message: "The government of Dr. Dollfuss has resigned. Dr. Rintelen has assumed power." Rintelen had come home from Rome for a few days and was in Vienna.

Before Dollfuss could leave the chancellory, 144 armed Nazis had seized it, barricading the doors.

1934

YOU SEE HOW SMALL HE WAS

by this picture of him with Mussolini, who himself is only 5 foot 6 inches high. Dollfuss had arranged to see Mussolini at the end of July and Austria's Nazis (as well as those in Germany) feared an agreement would be made between Austria and Italy, destroying hopes of joining up with Germany. Dollfuss was murdered in the chancellory. With a bullet in his throat he was allowed to lie on a couch and bleed to death. Nazis in the building waited in vain for Dr. Rintelen to come. He had been arrested. Their morale broke and at six in the evening, they filed out and were taken to the police barracks. Meanwhile, at the broadcasting studios, wires had been cut making it impossible for Nazis to transmit further messages. Police attacked and after a battle, entered the building. Here they are handing out wounded men from a window. The Nazi uprising failed.

DOLLFUSS HAD ☞

1934
—SHELLED THE SOCIALISTS

that year. Since 1918, the Socialist party had ruled the municipality of Vienna, even during the dictatorship of Dollfuss. They had made it a model city, though at great cost, and the Karl Marx House and Goethe House were two of the finest blocks of workers' flats in the world. But Vice-chancellor Major Fey, head of the Heimwehr, Austria's Fascists, had long been an enemy of the Socialists, and in February civil war broke out. All over the country there was fighting between Socialists and combined Government-Heimwehr forces. At the end of a week the Socialists were crushed, but nearly a thousand men, women and children had been killed and Vienna's model flats were in ruins (right), because Dollfuss had brought out artillery to shell the Socialists in them.

In Germany "The Purge"

Hitler's best friend was Captain Roehm (above), leader of the Brownshirt army which was becoming a burden on party finances, serving no useful purpose now Hitler was in power. Roehm wanted to transfer these Brownshirts into the Reichswehr, Germany's regular army, but Reichswehr chiefs were strongly opposed to this, and Hitler was in a quandary. Should he support Roehm and offend the Reichswehr or should he go against Roehm's wishes and cause probable discontent among his followers? One hundred thousand trained, fully armed men of the Reichswehr were more valuable to Hitler than 2,500,000 virtually unarmed, untrained Brownshirts. Hitler dropped Roehm. On the night of June 30, veteran members of Hitler's bodyguard went out, dragged Roehm from bed and later shot him. In twenty four hours more than two hundred men were murdered. Schleicher (see page 187) was shot at his home, so, too, was his wife. And when the "purge" was over, Hitler announced that the dead men were morally corrupt and had been planning to overthrow him.

While in England there was DROUGHT

"Use Less Water," was the slogan posted all over London in July. London's average rainfall during May and June is well over one-and-a-half inches, but this year only three-quarters of an inch had been measured in June, one-third of an inch in May. Drought hit other parts of the country even harder than London; reservoirs dried up, water supplies were cut off. One of the most seriously hit towns was Kettering, Northants., with its population of 33,000. Only three hours each day was its water-supply turned on. This shows the sun-baked bottom of one of the town's reservoirs in July.

1934

☛ AND MR. BELISHA

Minister of Transport, was voted by "Daily Express" readers in a ballot outstanding political figure of the year. Comments on Leslie Hore-Belisha (here opening a new $2\frac{1}{2}$ miles roadway at Greenford, Middlesex, in December) were: ". . . the man who had avoided tragedy by providing light comedy." ". . . the man who is watching our steps." Among Government measures to try to help bring down the yearly toll of more than 200,000 people killed and injured on roads, were 30 m.p.h. speed limits in built-up areas, and the prohibiting of car-hooting at night. But Hore-Belisha's most renowned (and most criticised) innovation was the setting-up of special road crossings for pedestrians, marked at each end by a "Belisha beacon"—a yellow globe on black and white post.

1934

AN ENGLISH WIMBLEDON

Dorothy Round and Fred Perry regained the men's and women's world tennis singles titles from America at Wimbledon in July, when Dorothy Round (below) beat the American champion Helen Jacobs (6-2, 5-7, 6-3), and Fred Perry (right) beat the Australian champion Jack Crawford (6-3, 6-0, 7-5). The last time Britain had won both titles had been in 1909, the year that both these British champions were born.

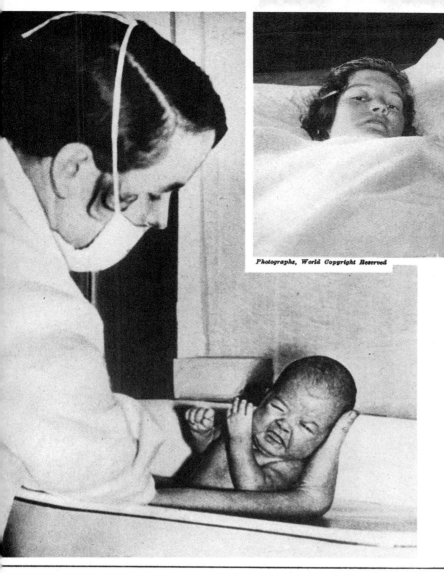

QUINS!

At four o'clock in the morning of May 28, Doctor Allan Dafoe, of Callender on the Canadian frontier, was called to 24-year-old Mrs. Elzize Dionne, who was expecting a baby. When he arrived, a baby girl had already been born, and within half an hour, four more daughters were born. (They weighed in all 10 lbs. 2¼ ozs., at their first weighing five days later.) A few hours after news of quintuplets (born only once in 57,000,000 births) had reached newspaper offices, reporters, photographers, nurses, an amusement promoter, gifts and most important of all, a paraffin-heated incubator arrived at the Dionne home. Dr. Dafoe and the incubator helped keep the quins alive, and soon the whole world was taking interest in them. The Canadian Government passed laws to protect them from exploitation.

AT LAST

they began to demolish Waterloo Bridge (see page 56)

at the end of June. Seven hundred of its granite balusters were offered to the public at £1 each, and cars, carts and barrows kept arriving at the still-open north end of the bridge to carry away the 2½ cwt. souvenirs. In October, Sir Giles Scott's revised design for a new bridge was adopted by the L.C.C. Highways Committee. £100,000 was to be cut off the scheme's original estimated cost of £1,295,000. Here is a view of the bridge in the last stages of demolition.

IT WAS IN 1934 THAT—

SIR WILLIAM MORRIS BECAME LORD NUFFIELD

New peer in the New Year's Honours List of 1934 was 56-year-old Sir William Morris, millionaire motor manufacturer and philanthropist, who had begun his career at 17 making bicycles on a capital of £5.

THE TRUNK BODIES WERE FOUND

On June 17, the torso of a young woman was found in a trunk at the cloakroom on Brighton station. Next day, the legs of a woman, presumably the same victim, were found in a suitcase at King's Cross. The following February, an open verdict was returned on the unknown woman victim of Brighton Mystery No. 1. On July 15, the body of Mrs. Saunders, 42-year-old dancer known as Violette Kay, was found in a trunk in the basement of a Brighton house. In this case, police arrested a waiter Jack Notyre, alias Tony Mancini, on a charge of murder, but after five days' trial in December, he was acquitted.

SIR GERALD DU MAURIER DIED

in London on April 11. Almost the last of the great actor-managers, he had been ill for many months with an internal complaint.

KING ALBERT WAS KILLED

by a fall from a 200 ft. crag on February 17 while climbing alone in the mountains forty miles from Brussels. This Belgian king—one of the heroic figures of the Great War—was succeeded by his son King Leopold (see page 225).

THE MORRO CASTLE CAUGHT FIRE

when on a cruise from Havana to New York in September, and from this 11,520-ton American liner only 85 people, mostly crew, put off in the six boats which could have held 408. The Morro Castle, still burning, drifted ashore (above) ; 134 people died and the ship became a total loss, claims being made against underwriters for £840,000.

1935: THE JUBILEE

Never before had London seen such celebrations as marked the ending on May 6 of King George V's twenty-five years' reign over 493,000,000 subjects. Again the capital was floodlit (see page 172), and hundreds of thousands of people thronged the streets not only at night but during the day. Decorations hung from every building, streets were lined with garlands. Here is part of Fleet Street, looking towards St. Paul's Cathedral. The black-glass building on left is the London office of the "Daily Express."

CROWDS ☞

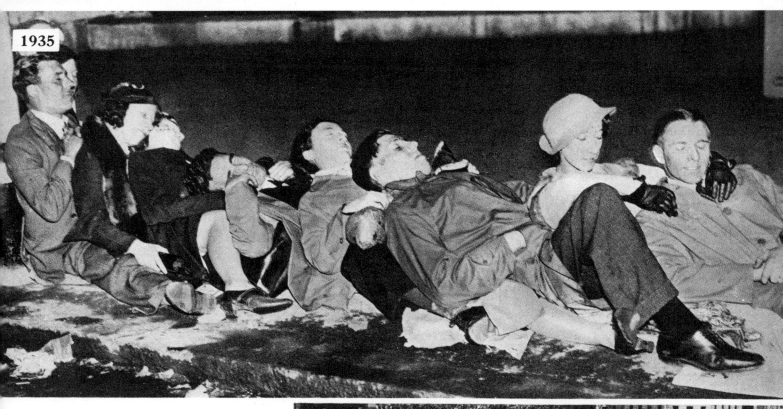

WAITED
ALL
NIGHT

for the procession on May 6, when King George V and Queen Mary rode in sunshine to St. Paul's Cathedral for the Jubilee Thanksgiving service. Temperature that day was 74 in the shade. Thousands sat and slept all along the route. (Here are some of them outside Buckingham Palace (above), and here is the scene at Trafalgar Square). Forty members of the Royal family and 4,000 leading citizens of Britain and the Empire attended the Cathedral service. That night, in his Empire broadcast speech, King George V said: "The Queen and I thank you from the depths of our hearts for the loyalty and—may I say?—the love with which this day and always you have surrounded us . . . To the children I would like to send a special message . . . I ask you to remember that in days to come you will be the citizens of a great Empire . . . and when the time comes, be ready and proud to give to your country the service of your work, your mind and your heart."

THEIR MAJESTIES ENTER THE CITY

At Temple Bar, the boundary of the City of London, the Royal carriage was held up at the point of a sword in accordance with ancient custom. (In 1642, Charles I violated parliamentary liberties by entering the House of Commons to seize five members for treason. They took refuge in the City and when Charles II came to the throne, it was laid down that the Sovereign should never cross the City boundaries except by permission of the Lord Mayor.) Also in accordance with ancient custom, the Lord Mayor, then Sir Stephen Killick, whose face is reflected in the polished side of the carriage, handed the hilt of the sword to the King, who then handed it back. The procession moved into the City.

ANOTHER ROYAL OCCASION

was on November 6, when the Duke of Gloucester (below) married Lady Alice Montague-Douglas-Scott (left), daughter of the late Duke of Buccleuch, in the chapel of Buckingham Palace. It was a quiet wedding, owing to the death of the bride's father on Oct. 19.

219

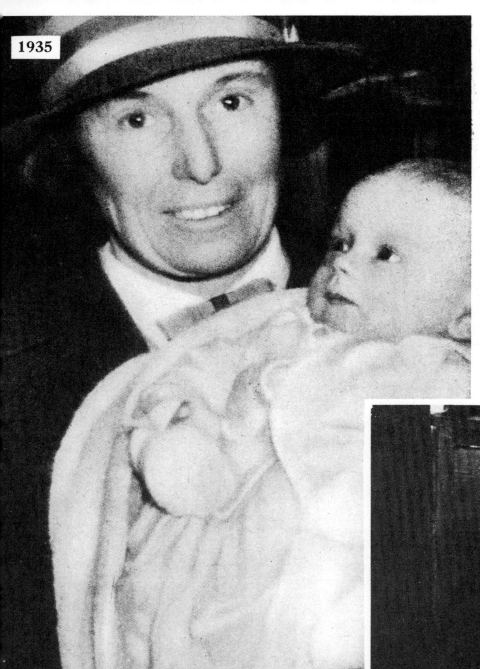

☞ A PRINCE IS BORN

m London on October 9. Son of the Duke and Duchess of Kent, the new prince weighed 6 lbs. 12 ozs. at birth, had light-blue eyes and fair hair which had a tendency to curl at the back. First prince to be born into the House of Windsor, that is, since King George V changed the Royal Family name from Wettin to Windsor in June 1917, he was christened Edward Nicholas George Paul Patrick the following month. Here he is on an outing at Christmas that year. Next year on Christmas Day, he got a 6½ lbs. blue-eyed, fair-haired sister who was christened six weeks later Alexandra Helen Elizabeth Olga Christabel.

IN ST. NEOTS: QUADS

At a council house in the little town of St. Neots, in Huntingdonshire, there came a letter from Buckingham Palace on December 2: "The Keeper of the King's Privy Purse is commanded by his Majesty to pay the King's Bounty to Mrs. Miles, and accordingly forwards herewith a cheque for £4." On November 29, three boys and a girl had been born to 33-year-old Mrs. Miles, and the following day they were christened Ann, Ernest, Paul and Michael.

ABYSSINIA INVADED

"Our future lies to the east and south, in Asia and Africa," Mussolini had told the Italian people. Italy with a population of forty two millions, increasing at the rate of 450,000 births yearly, needed more land for colonising. Mussolini too, needed political prestige ; his aim, ever since he had become dictator (see page 47), was to make Italy a great Power. In October Italy invaded Abyssinia, last remaining independent territory that had not been acquired by other European nations. Abyssinia's Emperor, Haile Selassie (here he is watching troops in the capital Addis Ababa), decided to fight back. His army was said to number two million men, though most of their weapons were primitive. They hoped to bring down enemy planes by rifle fire (picture below).

221

Their anti-aircraft was primitive

THE PROMISED LAND

was a region of dry plains, jungle and mountains, stretching over an area of 400,000 square miles, three times the size of Italy. But how valuable it was nobody quite knew. Coal, iron-ore, copper, gold, platinum and other minerals had been found in small quantities ; the British consul in his 1932 report, said : "It remains to be shown that there is in fact great mineral wealth awaiting profitable exploitation." In December 1934, an Italian military detachment camped at Wal Wal, well inside Abyssinian territory (though Italy denied this). Abyssinians attacked them and killed thirty-two. Mussolini demanded an apology, £20,000 indemnity and on October 3, in spite of League protests and threats of sanctions (by League members cutting off supplies), sent his troops into the country, under Generals Graziani, de Bono, Teruzzi and Pavone. They advanced steadily. (These photographs show an Italian advance post near Makale (right), and bearded Graziani with his officers (below) receiving homage of tribal chiefs after the fall of Adowa, which avenged the defeat there of 13,000 Italian troops in 1896.)

It was over Abyssinia that HOARE LOST HIS JOB

Eleven and a half million people in Britain voted in an informal plebiscite held in June by the League of Nations Union. More than ten million of the votes were in favour of non-military economic sanctions against Italy. It put Baldwin, who was Prime Minister at this time, in a quandary. He knew Germany was re-arming (Britain, France and Italy had met in conference at Stresa in April, and issued a declaration condemning German re-armament in defiance of the Versailles Treaty), yet he felt that public opinion would be against him if he advocated a policy of British re-armament. In November, when a general election was held, he gave pledges that the National Government would support the League of Nations and whatever was decided at Geneva. "You can trust me by now" he said. A National Government was returned to power with a majority of 250. In December, however, news leaked out from Paris that Sir Samuel Hoare, then Britain's Foreign Secretary, had met France's premier, Laval, to approve a plan that had been drawn up by them which involved the partition of Abyssinia between Mussolini and Selassie. There was public outcry against the plan. Baldwin, defending it in Parliament, said his lips were sealed, but if they were unsealed not a man would go into the lobby against him. The outcry grew and near the end of December, Hoare (right) was dropped as Foreign Secretary and Anthony Eden (left) took his place.

WIRED PICTURE

shows the crumpled wreck of "Flying Bird," the plane in which Wiley Post, one-eyed American airman, and Will Rogers, ex-cowboy film comedian, crashed in Northern Alaska on August 15 while on a flight attempt across the North Pole to Moscow. Pictures transmitted this way are put on a stationary cylinder, while a revolving beam of light passes over the picture, strip by strip. Reflected light passes into a photo-electric cell that causes impulses to be sent out which can be picked up by receiving stations thousands of miles away, and turned back into a dotted picture. One week later, the photographs (right), which had come by train and boat, arrived in England.

Wiley Post had twice flown round the world; in 1931 with Harold Gatty and in 1933, alone. Will Rogers was world-famed for his wise-cracks. He had last come to England in 1932. "When I go to London" he said, "I watch them changing the guard. When I go to Paris I watch them changing the Government."

👉 **Another lost airman was**

Sir Charles Kingsford Smith, 38-year-old Australian who was first man to fly round the world by direct routes over the Pacific and Atlantic. On November 6, with a fellow pilot J. T. Pethybridge, he set out from Lympne, Kent, on a last long-distance flight before taking up administrative work on Australian air mail and passenger services. They flew 4,800 miles in 1 day, 5 hours, 28 minutes, then took off for Singapore. They were never seen again and after search had been abandoned, were presumed dead in December.

224

QUEEN OF THE BELGIANS KILLED

Sitting beside her husband, King Leopold of the Belgians, on August 29, Queen Astrid (left) met the full force of impact as their car crashed into the rushes by the side of Lake Lucerne after it had plunged off the road. The Queen was thrown head-first against a tree; in two minutes she was dead. At the funeral service in Brussels, King Leopold (below) walked with his arm strapped to his side, his ribs in plaster. He had lost two stone in weight, looked haggard and pale. Though he staggered twice on the way to the service, he walked alone on the three-miles' journey from the church to the burial vaults.

This was the car—

On being examined, it was found that the bonnet and doors were torn away, the steering column broken. According to a statement ascribed to the King, the Queen was following the route on a map and he leaned over her to glance at it, taking his eyes off the road for a fraction of a second. At the same moment the car struck the kerb.

ON THE FRONT PAGES

RUXTON

Dismembered bodies of two women were found in a ravine near Moffat, Dumfrieshire on September 30, and Dr. Buck Ruxton, 36-year-old Indian was charged in connection with the crime.

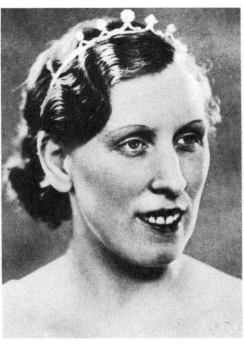

HIS WIFE

was missing for some days and her body was found to be one of those in the ravine. After eleven days trial, Ruxton was found guilty of the murder of his wife and servant, and sentenced to death. He failed in his appeal and was executed on May 12.

CAMPBELL

A tyre punctured in Sir Malcolm Campbell's 2,350 h.p. car "Blue Bird" when he was travelling at 280 m.p.h. on Bonneville Salt Flats Utah, U.S.A. in an attempt on the world's land speed record. Here he is examining the tyre On September 3, he set up a new world's record of 301.1 m.p.h. But at Utah, two years later George Eyston did 311.42 m.p.h.

JELLICOE

Eight Admirals, a Field Marshal, and an Air Marshal were pall-bearers at the funeral of 75-year-old Admiral of the Fleet Earl Jellicoe, who died in November. He lay in state at Westminster Abbey, first of the Great War leaders to be so honoured, then was buried near Nelson in the Crypt of St. Pauls on November 25.

KING OF GREECE

His twelve years of exile ended on November 3, when a Greek plebiscite showed a 90% Royalist vote. He returned on November 25, and despite opposition of Kondylis, the premier, who later resigned, declared an amnesty affecting 1,200 rebels, including a veteran Greek republican, M. Venizelos.

MRS. RATTENBURY

widow of a 67-year-old retired architect who died from head injuries at his home in May, was arrested with 19-year-old chaffeur George Stoner on charges of murder. After five days trial, Stoner was found guilty and sentenced to death. Mrs. Rattenbury was acquitted, but committed suicide on June 5. Stoner failed in an appeal, but was reprieved on June 25.

1936:
DEATH
OF
KING
GEORGE
THE
FIFTH

SANDRINGHAM. NORFOLK.

DEATH CAME PEACEFULLY TO THE KING

AT .11.55 p.m. TONIGHT, IN THE PRESENCE

OF HER MAJESTY THE QUEEN, THE PRINCE OF

WALES, THE DUKE OF YORK, THE PRINCESS

ROYAL, AND THE DUKE AND DUCHESS OF KENT.

(Signed) Frederic Willans,

Stanley Hewett,

Dawson of Penn.

20th January, 1936.

Villagers at Sandringham, Norfolk, worshipped with King George V in Sandringham Church on Sunday morning, January 11. In the afternoon, walking in his estate, he staggered and was helped back to Sandringham House. By Tuesday he was out again, riding a favourite white pony, but three days later came news that he was confined to his room with a cold. On Friday night it was announced that there were signs of heart weakness. Rapidly his condition grew worse, and on Monday January 20 came the news that all hope was gone. Round the royal bed at Sandringham House gathered the Prince of Wales, Duke of York, Duke of Kent, Archbishop of Canterbury, Home Secretary Sir John Simon, Lord President of the Council Ramsay MacDonald, Lord Chancellor Viscount Hailsham and Clerk of the Council Sir Maurice Hankey, ready to appoint a Council of State to act during his Majesty's illness. Sadly Britain and the Empire listened to the broadcast message at 9.25 : "The King's life is drawing peacefully towards its close ;" at 11.55, King George V died. The bulletin (above) was posted up at Sandringham; the flag on the church (left) next day flew at half-mast.

Long live the King:

cried Heralds on January 22, when they proclaimed the accession to the throne of King Edward VIII, who had been Prince of Wales. Here is Norroy King of Arms (Major A. H. Howard) reading the Proclamation at Temple Bar. The new King, at a Privy Council meeting said : "When my father stood here 26 years ago he declared that one of the objects of his life would be to uphold constitutional government. In this I am determined to follow in my father's footsteps." In Sandringham Church, thousands of people filed past the coffin of King George V which was guarded by four foresters ; on the 23rd of the month it was taken on a gun-carriage to the station. Behind the cortege walked (below, left to right) : the Duke of York, King Edward VIII, Duke of Kent, Duke of Gloucester and Lord Harewood.

THE LAST JOURNEY

In London, more than 800,000 people passed the bier during the four days' lying-in-state at Westminster Hall, and on January 28 unprecedented crowds, which had begun to gather before midnight the previous evening, watched in silence the final passing of King George V through the capital for burial at Windsor. At Marble Arch (above) and several other points, people were massed so deeply that police found it hard to keep the route clear. In the procession were the five kings of Belgium, Bulgaria, Denmark, Norway and Rumania, the President of the French Republic and representatives from every other country in the world.

THE McMAHON INCIDENT

As King Edward VIII was returning along Constitution Hill to Buckingham Palace on July 16, at the head of six battalions of the Guards to whom he had presented new colours in Hyde Park, a man, George McMahon, broke through the police cordon and a loaded revolver was thrown in the roadway. The King remained calm and rode straight on with only a glance at the scene (right) as the man was seized by police. (In the lower picture McMahon can be seen struggling near the St. John Ambulance by Hyde Park railings, while in the right-hand corner a police officer is dismounted, picking up the revolver.) McMahon came before Mr. Justice Greaves-Lord at the Old Bailey in September and the jury, after being absent for ten minutes, returned a verdict that McMahon was guilty on the charge of producing a revolver with intent to alarm the King. He was sentenced to twelve months' hard labour.

230

THE "NAHLIN" CRUISE

Climbing into his private airplane, piloted by Flight Lieut. "Mouse" Fielden, not long appointed Captain of the King's Flight, King Edward VIII left Heathrow airdrome, Middlesex, in August to begin a four-weeks' holiday. In fifty minutes the plane was across the Channel and the King then boarded a train that was to take him to the Dalmatian coast where millionairess Lady Yule's luxury yacht "Nahlin" (above) was waiting. King Edward had chartered the yacht to take him and fifteen guests on an Adriatic cruise.

Among the guests was a Mrs. Simpson

slender, dark-haired 39-year-old American who was married to a London business man. She had been married before—in 1916—to an American Naval officer Lieut. Earl W. Spencer, but had divorced him eleven years later and married Ernest Simpson in 1928. Soon after the Simpsons moved to London, and took a flat in Bryanston Square, W. They met the then Prince of Wales and by 1934, the Prince and Mrs. Simpson had become good friends.

SHE —

231

—BECAME THE MOST FAMOUS WOMAN IN THE WORLD

during the next few months. Few photographs of King Edward and Mrs. Simpson on the "Nahlin" cruise were published in Britain, but in other countries, particularly America, the pictures caused public comment. Twice after his return from the cruise, King Edward saw to it that Mrs. Simpson's name was printed in the Court Circular ; once at a dinner party which Mr. and Mrs. Baldwin attended, the other on the arrival of Mrs. Simpson with some guests at Balmoral. Then on October 27, a decree nisi was granted Mrs. Simpson at Ipswich Assizes, but only small paragraphs appeared in the British Press reporting this latest move of a woman the whole world was soon to be talking about.

The country had not heard of her until—

☛ ## DR. BLUNT BISHOP OF BRADFORD

spoke out on December 1 : "The King's personal views are his own but it is still an essential part of the idea of kingship . . . that the King needs the grace of God for his office." The public began to ask what the King had done to deserve this rebuke ; next day the Bishop said that he was not referring to any aspects of King Edward's private life, but simply that he did not seem to go to church enough ; on December 3 newspapers dropped their self-imposed censorship and began to tell their readers all about the matter.

THUS BEGAN THE ☛

CRISIS

It was not just the matter of King Edward's affection for a woman who had two former husbands living. It involved constitutional issues. Baldwin (right) on his own initiative had gone to the King on October 20, to tell him of his growing alarm at rumours which would, he thought, damage the Crown. On November 16, King Edward saw Baldwin again and said to the Prime Minister: "I am going to marry Mrs. Simpson and I am prepared to go." On November 20 they discussed possibility of Parliament passing a special Bill that would allow King Edward to marry Mrs. Simpson without her becoming Queen. Baldwin was told to put the matter before members of the Cabinet (up till then he had kept everything from his colleagues.) On December 2 Baldwin informed the King that although inquiries were not complete they had gone far enough to indicate that neither Britain nor the Dominions would tolerate a proposed morganatic marriage. King Edward accepted Baldwin's statement. Meanwhile, crowds gathered daily in Whitehall waiting for news. There were demonstrations against the Prime Minister (see cyclist's notice in picture on left) and against the Archbishop of Canterbury (lower right), head of the Church of England which was opposing the marriage on the divorce issue.

INSTRUMENT OF ABDICATION

I, Edward the Eighth, of Great Britain, Ireland, and the British Dominions beyond the Seas, King, Emperor of India, do hereby declare My irrevocable determination to renounce the Throne for Myself and for My descendants, and My desire that effect should be given to this Instrument of Abdication immediately.

In token whereof I have hereunto set My hand this tenth day of December, nineteen hundred and thirty six, in the presence of the witnesses whose signatures are subscribed.

SIGNED AT
FORT BELVEDERE
IN THE PRESENCE
OF

Edward RI

Albert

Henry

George

THE DECISION

was reached eight days after the December 2 meeting between King and Premier. King Edward sat up late at night at Fort Belvedere, Windsor (above), thinking over his great decision. He could keep the throne—and give up Mrs. Simpson ; he could ignore Baldwin's advice, ask for the Premier's resignation and rule with a new Cabinet ; or he could abdicate. On the evening of December 10 he decided on this last course.

ABDICATION

Witnessed by his three brothers, Duke of York, Duke of Gloucester, Duke of Kent, he signed the deed of abdication (left). The following afternoon Baldwin stood up in the House of Commons, nervously holding some papers. "A message from His Majesty the King, signed by His Majesty's own hand," he said, and handed the papers to Capt. Fitzroy, Speaker of the House. Then the news was read out that King Edward had given up the throne.

God save the King!

were the last words of Prince Edward when he spoke on the radio to millions of listeners on the night of December 11 before leaving in a closed car (above) for the destroyer "Fury" that was to take him from Portsmouth across the Channel into exile. "I want you to know that the decision I have made has been mine and mine alone" he said. "There has never been any constitutional difference between me . . . and Parliament . . . I should never have allowed any such issue to arise." His brother, formerly Duke of York had been proclaimed by Heralds (picture at left shows one of them at Temple Bar), and on December 12 the new King (below), leaving his home at 145 Piccadilly, held his Accession Council, declared his adherence to the strict principles of constitutional government and announced that the former king would henceforth be known as the Duke of Windsor.

235

Meanwhile in Spain—
WAR

Middle-class intellectuals formed the Republican government of Spain after the flight of King Alfonso in 1931 (see page 175). They believed they could alter things in Spain without revolution; but they faced opposition from Church, army and landowners. Forty thousand priests and clergy, all paid by the State, dominated Spanish life; though they controlled education, 45% of the people were illiterate. Church interests were bound with those of big landowners; 51% of Spain was owned by 1% of the population, Church property was valued at £100,000,000. One-quarter of the national budget went for Spain's army, most top-heavy in the world, with its seven hundred Generals and 21,000 officers (that is, one officer to every six men). To curb the power of landowners, army and Church, Spain's new government passed many laws but did little to enforce them, and when the government was forced out of office in 1933 a coalition of Rightist parties came to power. Strikes, riots and workers' revolts that broke out were crushed severely; by the end of 1935 thirty thousand socialists and republicans were in prison. In February came a general election. Republican parties joined up and got 4,839,449 votes; Rightists parties got 3,996,931 votes. Six months later, on July 18, the Rightists rose against the newly-elected government. Civil war had come to Spain.

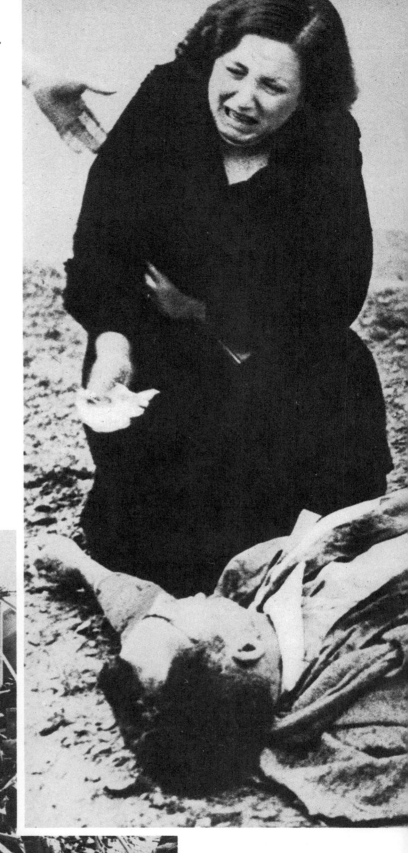

BOMBS

caused both these pictures. Madrid, capital of Spain, held by the government, had its first air raid on August 6, and within a few weeks planes were dropping bombs daily to wreck buildings (as at left).

ON YOUR RIGHT—FRANCO:
ON YOUR LEFT —AZANA

When garrisons all over Spain revolted on July 18 as planned, scholarly Manuel Azana who had been Prime Minister of the Republican government but was now Spain's president, called a meeting of Ministers and advised that all men under 30 should be mobilised. In more important cities, Madrid, Barcelona, Valencia, Malaga, Bilbao, the revolts were crushed. Plans to overthrow the government of Spain in a single night failed. But the Governor of the Canary Isles, short, paunchy General Franco, a soldier who at 34 had been youngest general in the Spanish army, ruined all hopes of future peace. He flew overnight to take leadership of rebel troops in Spanish Morocco and soon had them across the Straits of Gibraltar to fight in southern Spain.

In Palestine FIGHTING

Resentful of the plan made under the terms of Britain's League of Nations mandate for a Jewish National Home, Palestine's 1,000,000 Arabs had long been antagonistic to the 400,000 Jews there, and in April trouble broke out at Jaffa, when Arabs and Jews met in armed conflict. It was the start of seven months' rioting, ambushes and sabotage in which British troops were needed to impose order. During that time 37 members of the defence forces, 82 Jews and more than 1,000 Arabs lost their lives.

In Abyssinia
ADDIS ABABA
TAKEN

At the end of seven months' fighting, with nearly half a million soldiers in Abyssinia, Italy annexed the country after troops had marched into Addis Ababa (say it : ABB-abber) on May 5. Abyssinians had rioted and looted the town. (Some of them are lying dead in the picture above, while an Italian soldier stands guard in the main street.)

☛ THE NEGUS

three days before this had fled and embarked on a British cruiser which took him to Palestine. He came to London in June. (Here he is with his daughter, solemn Princess Tsahai, on the balcony of his London residence.) "I do not intend to settle in England," he said. "I still dream and hope of returning to Abyssinia. At present I have not the means." Mussolini too, was having money trouble. It had cost him more than £33,000,000 to prepare for war ; at least £126,000,000 to fight it. But he said : "Italy has at last her Empire—a Fascist Empire."

MAIDEN VOYAGE

of the Queen Mary (see page 171), began on May 27 from Southampton, under the command of Sir Edgar Britten. "We are not out to beat the record" he said "but we may do it." Though they failed, a grand welcome awaited when the Queen Mary reached New York (above). Thousands of New Yorkers paid 4/- a time to look around her; left with ash-trays, silverware and plates as souvenirs. In August, the Queen Mary made two record-breaking trips and got back from France's Normandie the Blue Riband of the Atlantic. She crossed from New York in 3 days 23 hours 57 minutes. On October 28, just before he was due to sail, Sir Edgar had a seizure and died soon after. The Normandie regained the Blue Riband early the following year.

CRYSTAL PALACE BURNT

This picture (left) shows the still-smouldering ruins of London's £1,500,000 amusement centre and landmark, the Crystal Palace, which was destroyed by fire on November 30. Within half an hour of the first alarm the building, covering twenty-five acres, was wholly ablaze and the glow from the flames could be seen eighty miles away. Investigation failed to find the cause of the fire.

RESIGNED

A Tribunal making public inquiry into alleged Budget leakages causing undue losses to Lloyds' underwriters, found that there was unauthorised disclosure of Budget information by J. H. Thomas, then Colonial Secretary, to Sir Alfred Butt, M.P. and Alfred Bates, London business man. Both J. H. Thomas and Sir Alfred Butt resigned their seats in Parliament.

SOLO

First woman to fly solo across the Atlantic from east to west was Mrs. Beryl Markham, who left Abingdon, Berks., on September 4, and made a forced landing safely in Nova Scotia the following day.

GENERAL

Outnumbered four to one by 42 German divisions in March 1918, the Fifth Army, under General Sir Hubert Gough, fell back for eight days. Gough was relieved of his command. Eighteen years later, in November, Lloyd George who was Premier during the Great War, publicly vindicated the general. "You were completely let down" he said. "No general could have won that battle."

"KIM"

Rudyard Kipling, 70-year-old story teller and poet of Empire, died after an operation on January 18. He began his career as newspaper reporter in India; said to an editor of the "Daily Express" years later: "I wish I could have remained a reporter."

BOY KING

King Fuad of Egypt, world's richest king, (his fortune was £10,000,000), died in April after several teeth had been extracted. His 16-year-old son Farouk, who was staying in Surrey, hurried home to Cairo and on April 28 was proclaimed King of Egypt.

MYSTERY MAN

Eighty-seven year old Greek Sir Basil Zaharoff, mystery armaments-salesman, died from a heart attack in November. He made £30,000,000 profit out of the Great War; had 298 decorations given him by thirty-one nations.

1937 : CORONATION

The Coronation of George VI in Westminster Abbey, crowning place since William the Conqueror of 37 English kings, called for 25,000 police and 8,000 special constables who were needed to handle more than ten million people who had thronged to London to see the world's greatest free show ; over which, it was estimated, £40,000,000 changed hands. Most expensive Coronation on record, its cost to the State was nearly £500,000, its preparations lasted more than six months. At 10.30 in the morning, the not very comfortable golden royal coach (above), with the King and Queen inside, left Buckingham Palace.

IT WAS—

MAY THE TWELFTH

In Westminster Abbey, peers and peeresses, who had been in their 19-inch-wide seats before nine o'clock, tried to conceal as best they could sandwiches and drinks they had brought with them; many using coronets (minimum cost £16) as sandwich boxes. Outside the Abbey, crowds packed behind the lines of 40,000 fighting men along the route, cheered at the six-miles-long procession with its Royalties in glass carriages, distinguished men and women from every country in the world, soldiers, sailors, airmen, bands and prancing horses preceding the golden coach. (Here is part of the procession at Admiralty Arch, by Trafalgar Square.)

LONDON WALKED

to see the Coronation. At midnight on April 30, London's 260,000 busmen had come out on strike after negotiations for a 7½-hour day had broken down. Fine weather helped ease the plight of bus-users during the 27 days when the busmen were out. London's 4,700 buses were less missed than they might have been, as traffic congestion around May 12 was at its worst.

THE CROWNING

was done by 72-year-old Dr. Cosmo Gordon Lang, £15,000 a year Primate of All England. Immediately after, the hundreds of peers and peeresses put on their own coronets and everybody in the Abbey cried: "God Save the King." Guns at the Tower of London and all over Britain were fired to mark this moment. At 4 in the afternoon, the King and Queen were back at Buckingham Palace. (Picture above shows them on the balcony with Princess Elizabeth and Princess Margaret Rose. The King is wearing the State Crown, not the heavy St. Edward's Crown placed on his head at Westminster Abbey). That night he broadcast to the Empire, first time in history that a newly-crowned king had talked to his peoples in their own homes.

NEXT MONTH —

on the fourth, at the Château de Candé near Tours in France, the Duke of Windsor married Mrs. Simpson, whose divorce had been made absolute the first week in May. No member of the royal family was among the sixteen guests, but the 60-year-old vicar of Darlington, Rev. J. A. Jardine, against the wishes of the Archbishop of Canterbury, was there. Writing privately to the Duke a week before, he had been invited to officiate at the ceremony. After the wedding, the Duke and Duchess of Windsor, who had got more than 3,000 congratulatory telegrams and 30,000 letters, left for a honeymoon in Austria.

THEY MET HITLER

in October at his mountain villa in Berchtesgaden, near the Austrian frontier. While the Duchess chatted with Nazi leaders, the Duke had a twenty-minutes' private conversation with Germany's dictator. Criticism followed this action in making Germany first country of visit in a tour the Duke of Windsor had planned to study social conditions. But early in November in the first public speech since leaving England, he told newspaper men in Paris that he was mystified by the ulterior motives attributed to his activities. "Though one may be in the lions' den," he said, "it is possible to eat with the lions if on good terms with them."

JAPAN INVADES CHINA

Without formal declaration of war, Japan invaded China in July after Chinese had fired on Japanese soldiers engaged on manœuvres near the Manchukuo frontier (see page 200). But China's resistance was greater than the Japanese had come to expect. Chiang Kai-Shek (see page 90), had become China's dictator and had built up a disciplined, well-equipped army. His wife Mei-Ling (upper right), American-educated Methodist member of China's ruling House of Soong, took over the organisation of propaganda, acted as news-censor, and negotiated, through her influential family, foreign loans. At Shanghai on August 28, sixteen Japanese planes bombed the area round Shanghai South Station, killing 200 people. This baby (right) crying amid the ruins was filmed by a Chinese cameraman, and it is estimated that 136,000,000 people all over the world saw the scene in newspapers and newsreels.

THE PANAY INCIDENT

Early on Sunday afternoon, December 12, Japanese planes swooped down to bomb the U.S. gunboat Panay that was steaming along the Yangtze River with refugees from Nanking, China's capital. For twenty minutes Panay seamen fired away with old Lewis guns (left), but the planes kept in line of the sun, so blinding the gunners. In two hours, the Panay sank and 54 survivors who had got to the river-bank lay hid in the rushes till planes, which had machine-gunned them as they left the ship, flew off. (Below is Quartermaster John Lang who had severe chin and arm wounds.)

JAPAN WAS "VERY SORRY"

Hirosi Saito, Japan's ambassador to the United States, offered immediate apologies when he heard the news. Though protesting that the bombing was "completely accidental" he called it a "terrible blunder." Soon after, from Tokyo, came offers of full compensation and a promise to punish offenders.

Baldwin hands over to Chamberlain

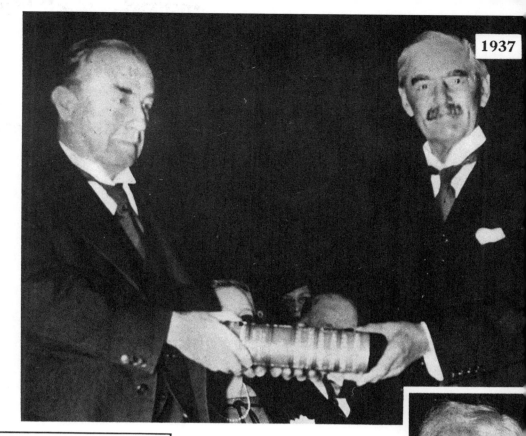

For many months, Stanley Baldwin had been planning to retire from political life, but events before and after King Edward's abdication had kept him in office. As soon as King George VI had been crowned, Baldwin decided to hand over the Premiership to Neville Chamberlain (see page 50), who was Chancellor of the Exchequer, and on May 28 the Chamberlain household moved in to No. 10 Downing Street where Baldwin and his wife Lucy had lived, on and off, for eight years. The former Prime Minister went into the House of Lords as Earl Baldwin of Bewdley. (Here he is at his first public appearance after taking the title, being given a presentation gift by Neville Chamberlain.).

ANOTHER PREMIER DIED

At 8.45 on November 9, 71-year-old Ramsay MacDonald (see page 62), who in his career had been pacifist, radical, Labour champion, Britain's first Socialist prime minister and first National Government prime minister, died from heart attack in mid-Atlantic while on the way to South America for a rest. A suggestion of burial in Westminster Abbey was made but he was buried at Lossiemouth, where he had been born.

☛PRINCESS JULIANA MARRIED

Wearing no make-up, Holland's Crown Princess Juliana (left) married Germany's Prince Bernhard, at The Hague on January 7. Prince Bernhard's action in becoming a naturalised Dutch subject just before this nearly caused a diplomatic incident between Germany and Holland. The Nazi prince who was to have been best man, stayed home through "illness"; and a German princess-bridesmaid stayed home because police would not give her a passport.

S T A R S . . .

Jean Harlow

(above) 26-year-old American film star, best known for her "platinum - blonde" bleached hair which started a vogue among hundreds of thousands of girls, died from uremia at her home in Beverley Hills, Hollywood on June 7.

Another Jean—Jean Batten

(top right) landed in her 200 h.p. Percival Gull monoplane at Croydon Airport on Sunday afternoon October 24, after having made her second Australia-England flight in the record time of 5 days, 18 hours, 15 minutes.

N.B. 1937 WAS THE YEAR—

when Oxford, for the first time since 1923, beat Cambridge in the Boat Race. Here is the Oxford crew passing the finishing post, three lengths ahead.

LAST FLIGHT

In a £20,000 Lockheed Electra plane (above), a "flying laboratory," Amelia Earhart (see page 113) set out from Miami, Florida, on June 1 to make a round-the-world flight. South America, Africa, India and Batavia—all were reached and Amelia Earhart began the last stages to tiny Howland Island, mid-Pacific air base. She was never seen again; and after intensive search, was presumed dead.

HINDENBURG BLOWS UP
After her first transatlantic crossing of the season, Germany's huge airship Hindenburg, biggest ever built, nosed down to the airdrome at Lakehurst, New Jersey on the evening of May 6.   A severe thunderstorm had just ended.   Landing lines were dropped, the ground crew began pulling her towards the mooring mast, when suddenly flames burst from her tail.   In a few seconds the Hindenburg, filled with 6,700,000 cubic feet of inflammable hydrogen, was on fire ; she began to buckle in the middle and fell to the ground (above).   Passengers and crew jumped for their lives as flames and explosions destroyed the airship.   In five minutes the fire had burned out, leaving 35 dead amid the wreckage. American pilots Dick Merrill and Jack Lambie, who flew the Atlantic to get Coronation pictures to fly back with, brought with them exclusive pictures of this disaster for the "Daily Express."

1938: DAUGHTER FOR JULIANA

Dutch doctors had predicted that Juliana's baby would be born not later than January 16; but it was not until the 31st, one year 24 days after the wedding (see page 247), that Holland learnt that a 7 lbs. 11 oz. baby, with fair hair and sky-blue eyes, had been born into the House of Orange-Nassau, rulers of the Netherlands since 1579; a princess who one day may rule over 69,000,000 people of the Netherlands and its possessions.

☞ This Picture

was a world scoop for the "Daily Express." The baby was only one day old. Even Dutch newspapers were unable to publish photographs until, several hours after it was published, air-mail copies of the "Daily Express" arrived in Amsterdam. Fourteen weeks later, on May 12, the baby was christened Beatrix Wilhelmina Armgaard.

KING FAROUK MARRIED

On January 20, Egypt's 17-year-old King Farouk (see page 240), clasped hands with his prospective father-in-law and promised to accept 16-year-old Farida Zulficar (right) as his wife. Then he handed over an envelope of money, signed three marriage contracts, and the wedding, conforming with Mohammedan custom, was over. Queen Farida had watched it from a latticed window; six hours later, she put on wedding dress and strolled through the Royal palace gardens to the music of Lohengrin's wedding march.

EDEN RESIGNS

Prime Minister Neville Chamberlain had decided to go forward with a proposed Anglo-Italian agreement, without terms, so easing the bad feeling between Italy and Britain that had started when Mussolini invaded Abyssinia (see page 221). Foreign Secretary Anthony Eden, however, firm believer in a League of Nations policy, was convinced that Mussolini first should be required to withdraw Italian troops fighting under General Franco's command in Spain (see page 237). The Cabinet threatened to split on this issue but on February 20, Eden (here he is with his wife Beatrice) resigned.

HONOUR FOR "GRACIE"

In the New Year's Honours List of 1938 it was announced that a Mrs. Grace Selinger had become a Commander of the Order of the British Empire; in plain English, "Gracie Fields got a C.B.E." Britain's highest-paid film and stage star, she went to Buckingham Palace on February 16 and said, when she came out (right): "I never felt so nervous in all my life. It's grand when you know you are to be presented to the King, but your knees do knock when the time comes."

SINKING OF THE BALEARES

Seventy miles off the coast of Cartagena, Spain, a Loyalist fleet of four destroyers and two cruisers met a Rebel fleet of four destroyers and three cruisers, shortly after midnight on March 6. First major naval battle since 1916, it ended at 2.30 a.m. with the sinking of the 10,000-ton Rebel cruiser Baleares by a Loyalist torpedo. Ignoring shouts to jump overboard from sailors on the British destroyer Kempenfelt that had come to the rescue, five hundred of the Baleares crew, including the admiral in command, were burned to death aboard the blazing cruiser. Rebel ships and British vessels picked up the rest of the 200-odd survivors. (Men swimming from the Baleares can be seen in lower left corner of the picture at right.)

HOW THE PICTURES
REACHED LONDON

Picture of the sinking of the Baleares (above) was one of several exclusive "Daily Express" pictures. Taken by the gunnery officer of the British destroyer Kempenfelt, they were handed to Noel Monks, "Daily Express" reporter, at Gibraltar. There were no radio facilities there so Monks chartered a tug to take him across the Mediterranean to Tangier in Morocco. At Tangier he chartered special planes to get the pictures to Marseilles, and there they were wired direct to the "Daily Express" London office, and so through to other offices in Manchester and Glasgow. Air view picture (left) was taken from a Spanish Loyalist plane.

GARBO AND STOKOWSKI

Standing high on the rocks above the Bay of Naples at Ravello, a lonely villa became news-centre in March. Thirty-one-year-old Swedish cinema actress, Greta Garbo, almost the only Hollywood star who had not even been married once, had come there with 56-year-old Leopold Stokowski, world-famed musical conductor to whom, it was rumoured, she was engaged. At last it seemed that Garbo, who always "wanted to be alone," was to share her solitude. Newspaper reporters gathered to hear the news, but on March 17 she sent for them all and said : "I am not married and I am not planning to marry. I never had any impulse towards the altar." Here she is (right) wearing cardigan and trousers in the grounds of the villa and (below) sightseeing in Rome—followed by Stokowski.

UHREN P. LADST

ANSCHLUSS

Since his youth, Hitler had dreamed of an Austro-German Anschluss—economic union between the two countries. Despite the warnings of his military advisers, despite objections raised by Dr. Schacht, expert economist, Hitler judged that Germany could take over Austria in March without being involved in war. Months of propaganda and diplomatic intrigue had prepared the ground for a bloodless invasion. Hitler's political instinct seemed sound again. Cheers greeted German troops as they arrived over the frontier and came into Austrian towns (above). Swastikas hung from windows, crowds gave the Nazi salute ; buttonholes, not bullets, greeted the marching men as they penetrated further into the land where Hitler was born.

MORE FLIGHT RECORDS
—New Zealand and Back

Bearded, cold and tired, Flying Officer A. E. Clouston and "Daily Express" Air Reporter Victor Ricketts climbed out of their 4-year-old Comet racing monoplane, Australian Anniversary, on Saturday evening, March 26, at Croydon Airdrome. In three hours under eleven days they had flown 28,000 miles from England to New Zealand and back. Among the ten records they had set up was the first direct round trip, England - New Zealand - England.

ACROSS THE ATLANTIC "BY MISTAKE"

Strangest flight on record ended at Baldonnel Airport, ten miles from Dublin, when 31-year-old American, Douglas Corrigan, climbed out of an oil-spattered plane and told airport officials he had just flown the Atlantic "by mistake." Twenty-nine hours before, friends had watched him leave New York for what was to be a 3,200 miles non-stop flight across America to Los Angeles. When he headed east out to sea they thought he was making a wide turn before heading west. But he kept straight on and—when the Atlantic was crossed—stuck to his story that he had flown it in error.

ROUND THE WORLD

Howard Hughes, American millionaire film producer, with four companions, landed at Floyd Bennett Airport, New York, in their big 14-seater Lockheed airliner on July 14, after having flown nearly 15,000 miles round the world in ninety-one hours. Through rain and fog, through winds and mists, they had kept up an average speed of more then 200 miles an hour, at a cost of £4 a mile. Their route had been New York to Paris, then to Moscow, across Siberia, across Canada and back to New York.

ROYAL VISIT TO PARIS

Ten thousand newly-released pigeons soared into the sky, "God Save the King" crashed out from hundreds of loud-speakers, guns began booming a 101-gun salute as the King and Queen arrived in Paris, on Tuesday, July 19, on the first State visit by British Royalty for twenty-four years. In open cars, behind a 2 ft. 6 in. screen of bullet-proof glass, they drove with President and Madame Lebrun along the four-mile route to their apartments at the Palais D'Orsay. Gardes Republicaine, with red-plumed helmets, dark-blue tunics and white breeches massed round the Royal cars (right). For four days France feted the King and Queen. (Here they are at a garden party with President and Madame Lebrun at the Chateau Bagatelle, on the outskirts of Paris.) When they left, at the end of their stay, Madame Lebrun's last words to them were: "You are taking away the hearts of all Paris with you."

World's Biggest Ship

Two hundred and fifty thousand people lined the banks of the Clyde on September 27, to see Queen Elizabeth launch a sister-ship to the Queen Mary (see page 239). This new Cunarder was to be the world's biggest liner; 85,000 tons displacement and 10 ft. longer than the Queen Mary. "I name this ship Queen Elizabeth and wish success to her and all who sail in her" said the Queen. Princess Margaret Rose, awed, and Princess Elizabeth, pleased, looked on as the ship (top right) slid smoothly down the runways and into the water.

350.2 M.P.H.

Thirty-eight year old City fur broker, John Cobb, driving his 2,500 h.p. Napier-Railton car on Bonneville Salt Flats, Utah, U.S.A. on September 15, raised the world land-speed record to 350.2 m.p.h. Britain's motor-racing heavyweight (he weighs 14 stone) had become the first man on earth ever to go faster than 350 m.p.h. in a car.

364 RUNS

Leonard Hutton, 22-year-old Yorkshire cricketer, batted for thirteen-and-a-half hours in the final England-Australia Test Match at the Oval in August. As runs mounted, excitement grew; then, a cut to the boundary (shown above) caused pandemonium among the crowd of 30,000. They cheered and sang and shouted; for Hutton had beaten Bradman's record of 334 (see page 153). Hutton made 364 runs before he was caught out by Hassett.

357.5 M.P.H.

But the following day, 41-year-old Captain George Eyston, tall, lean Londoner, drove his seven-ton, 6,000 h.p. Rolls-Royce car, Thunderbolt, at 357.5 m.p.h. over the same course, and so recaptured the measured mile and measured kilometre world records he had lost to John Cobb.

TENSION IN EUROPE

Czechoslovakia, carved out of the former Austro-Hungarian Empire, had been set up as an independent State in the heart of Europe at the end of the Great War. Within its boundaries, the treaty-makers had put 14,700,000 citizens ; nearly half of them Czechs, 3,200,000 Germans, 2 million Slovaks, 700,000 Hungarians, 600,000 Russians and 80,000 Poles. Czech President, Dr. Benes (shown below; his name is pronounced Ben-esh), had promised in 1919 that the Government of this new State of Czechoslovakia would take the Swiss Republic as a model. His Government, he said, would respect the rights of the country's different nationalities.

As the years passed, the Germans, largest minority in the State, complained they were not getting fair treatment. Marked preference, they said, was being shown to Czechs in the Army and Civil Service ; Czechs were getting business orders that had formerly gone to Germans. The State was, in fact as well as name, said the Germans, a Czechoslovak Republic. After seven years' agitation, reforms were promised ; German Social Democrats entered the Government ; things seemed brighter. Then came the world-wide industrial depression, hitting worst of all the industrial German districts south of the Sudeten Mountains, which marked Czechoslovakia's frontier with Germany. Factories closed down, thousands of people, unemployed, faced ruin. Plump, anti-Socialist, Konrad Henlein (above), a gymnasium instructor, began to echo the grievances of these Sudeten Germans ; quickly, he gathered supporters of his aims. Only eighteen months after he had formed his Sudeten German Homeland Party, he had gained forty-four seats in Parliament, 60% of the German votes. For a time Henlein kept declaring his loyalty to the Czechoslovakian State. But across the frontier Hitler was demanding : "One people, one State, one leader." In April, 1938, Henlein went to Berlin to see Hitler.

HENLEIN DEMANDS

When Henlein returned from his visit to Hitler, he rejected Czech offers of a charter of rights for minorities in Czechoslovakia, and at Carlsbad, on April 24, put forth his demands. He wanted full self-government for all German areas, full equality of status, reparation for all losses and damage suffered by the Germans in Czechoslovakia since 1918. The Czech Government refused to negotiate on these terms but said they were willing to discuss the whole minorities problem. Meantime, German troops were moving up guns (as seen here) to the Czech frontier. On May 21, the Czechs called up army reserves.

RUNCIMAN MEDIATES

So serious seemed the situation in July, that the Prime Minister announced in the House of Commons that Lord Runciman would go to Czechoslovakia as unofficial mediator between the Czech Government and the Sudeten Germans. This picture shows Lord Runciman's Mission in Prague ; left to right : Mr. G. Peto, formerly Lord Runciman's Parliamentary Secretary ; Lord Runciman ; Mr. F. Ashton-Gwatkin, of the Foreign Office ; Mr. Ian Henderson, of the Consular Service.

SIMON SPEAKS

In spite of the Runciman Mission, the situation grew worse during August. Both sides took up uncompromising attitudes ; the Czech Government made offers but felt all the time that they were negotiating, not with Henlein, but with Hitler. Europe waited to hear Britain's attitude, and on August 27, Sir John Simon made a speech at Lanark (right). It was guarded ; it reaffirmed British policy as defined by the Prime Minister in March— Britain could give no guarantee to go to the aid of Czechoslovakia or France if Czechoslovakia was attacked ; but if war broke out, it was impossible to assume that Britain would not become involved.

THESE SPEECHES SHOOK THE WORLD

In the days following Sir John Simon's speech at Lanark, the British Ambassador in Berlin, Sir Nevile Henderson, was called home to consult with the British Government upon the German attitude; Lord Runciman saw Henlein; Henlein met President Benes and then went to see Hitler. On September 4, the Czech Cabinet agreed on far-reaching concessions to the Sudeten Germans; they could have their full rights as a racial group; they could have administrative charge of local services such as health, education, local finance and police. But these concessions, said the Czech Cabinet, were the final limit. Three days later, Henlein broke off negotiations because of alleged incidents in a Sudeten German district; a Czech policeman had struck a Sudeten M.P. with a whip. Tension increased; the French took special measures on their north-east frontier because of big German troop movements there.

Then, on September 12, Hitler got up to speak at the Nazi Congress in Nuremberg (right). He attacked Dr. Benes and the Czechs, he threatened war and demanded self-determination (a nation's right to determine its own form of civil government) for the Sudeten Germans. Two weeks later, before 20,000 Nazis in the Sports Palace, Berlin, he cried: "Our patience is at an end . . . Benes must surrender his territory on October 1." (Here he is acknowledging the cheers; from left to right: Dr. Goebbels, Hitler, Rudolph Hess, General Goering, von Ribbentrop, Dr. Frick.)

1938

"October 1st"

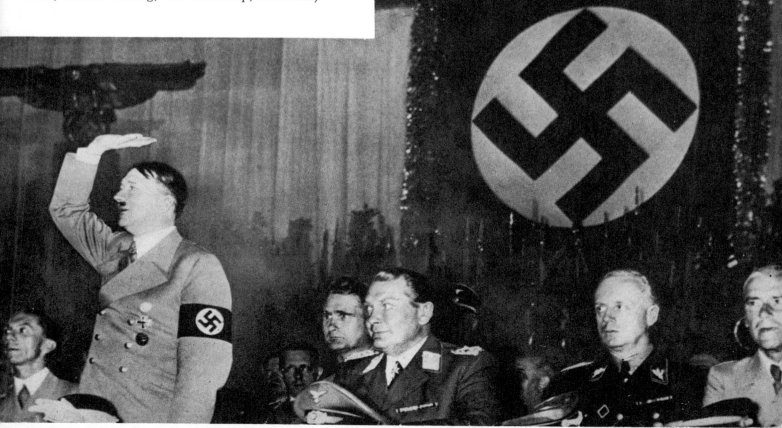

1938

TWO SIDES

In thickly populated Sudeten areas near the frontier, Henlein followers, armed with rifles, banded themselves into "Free Corps," ready to fight, if necessary, in guerilla warfare against Czech troops, to further Nazi aims. But not all Sudeten Germans relished Nazi rule ; though they had grievances against the Czech Government they were satisfied to settle their affairs in their own country without outside help. They resented Hitler's interference, they suspected his motives. Here are unarmed anti-Nazi demonstrators (below) marching through the Sudeten German area in Western Bohemia.

His First Flight

PREMIER VISITS HITLER

Two days after Hitler had spoken at Nuremberg, with Sudeten German districts under martial law, with troops massed along frontiers and all Europe expecting a seeming inevitable war, hopes of peace came unexpectedly and dramatically. Britain's Prime Minister, 69-year-old Neville Chamberlain, sent a message to Hitler that he would like to see him. Hitler replied favourably and the next day, September 15, Neville Chamberlain, who had never flown before, climbed into an airplane at Heston, to visit Hitler in his mountain chalet at Berchtesgaden in the Bavarian Alps. He was smiling, almost grinning, as he climbed out of the plane at the end of this trip. (Here he is being met by German Foreign Minister, von Ribbentrop). But talking to Hitler over the tea-table at Berchtesgaden (below) he found little cause to smile. (On Chamberlain's right is von Ribbentrop; facing the camera is moustached Sir Nevile Henderson; others in the group are interpreters and advisers).

THE MEETING AT BERCHTESGADEN

In this first interview, Chamberlain found Hitler adamant. He returned next day to London. The French Premier, M. Daladier, and Foreign Minister, M. Bonnet, flew over to draw up new proposals; they recommended the cession to Germany of Sudeten German areas, new frontiers to be marked by an international commission. Under diplomatic pressure the Czech Government accepted, and on September 22, Chamberlain again flew to Hitler, met him at Bad Godesburg, on the Rhine, and laid the Anglo-French proposals before him. The new plan was unacceptable to Hitler. As Chamberlain left after this second meeting (see next page) his face showed his disappointment.

A.R.P.

Monday Morning, Sept. 26

was the time when thousands of ordinary, peace-loving men and women in Britain first realised how near were the dangers of war. As they went to work that morning they saw sandbags being unloaded on the pavement outside office buildings; bills were being pasted up on walls; heavy black type listed places where gas masks were being distributed. Men had started digging in the parks (above), making trenches on spots which only a week before had borne notices: Keep Off the Grass. Plans for evacuating London's 600,000 children were being put into operation; first parties of invalids and very young children had begun to arrive at the main railway stations (below). In every part of the country, active work on Britain's air-raid precautions had started.

He holds her hand reassuringly as they wait for news in Parliament-square.

CROWDS WAITED —

outside the House of Commons on Wednesday, September 28, watching Members of Parliament arrive to hear the Prime Minister's statement on the crisis. British Naval Reserves had been called up that morning; several London Tube stations had been closed suddenly for important structural alterations; President Roosevelt had sent from America two peace appeals to Hitler.

JUST IN CASE . . .

Keepers and hostesses from the Children's Zoo took time off from their normal duties to fill sandbags for air-raid precautions at London's Zoo in Regent's Park.

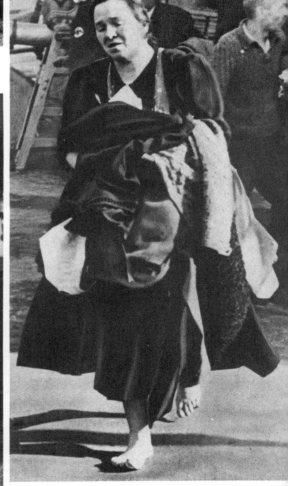

600 Miles away

this woman, barefooted, carrying her belongings, had arrived in Germany after crossing the frontier with hundreds of other fleeing Sudeten German refugees.

Forty million gas masks, costing 2/6 each, were being distributed free. This was a typical scene as voluntary workers measured up men, women and children for their proper-sized gas mask—large, medium or small.

The Big Four meet at Munich

When the Prime Minister rose in the House of Commons on Wednesday, September 28, the densely-packed members of Parliament cheered and clapped in wild enthusiasm; as he began to speak, diplomats and peers, in the crowded galleries above, craned to hear his words. For an hour and a half the House listened as he unfolded the story of the past few months; telling how he had gone direct to Hitler, how deadlock seemed to have been reached. Then quietly, near the end of his speech, the Prime Minister mentioned his "last, last effort for peace." In the early hours of that morning, he said, he had written two letters; one to Mussolini, one to Hitler, urging a conference by Britain, France, Germany and Italy to see if some agreement could be reached before war broke out. Mussolini was willing to co-operate; a note, handed to the Prime Minister as he was making his speech, told that Hitler was willing, too. In wild applause, the House adjourned; early the following morning, Neville Chamberlain once more climbed into a plane and flew to Munich. Mussolini had arrived there by train (left); in the afternoon, the four statesmen (shown here; left to right: Chamberlain, Daladier, Hitler, Mussolini) went into conference.

1938

Peace

"This bears Herr Hitler's name and mine . . . ."

At 12.30 on Friday morning, September 30, only twenty-three hours before Hitler's war ultimatum was to have expired, the four statesmen reached agreement on the Czechoslovak problem. Hitler's troops would occupy Sudeten areas in progressive stages, completing the occupation by October 10; an international commission would decide territories in which plebiscites would be held; Britain and France would guarantee the new frontiers of Czechoslovakia; Germany and Italy would join in this guarantee when all questions had been settled. On Friday evening the Prime Minister left for home; at Heston (right), to the crowds waiting to cheer him, he read out a pact, signed by himself and Hitler, that England and Germany should never again go to war.

This map shows approximately the areas of occupation in Czechoslovakia as agreed on by the four statesmen at Munich:

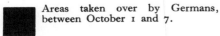 Areas taken over by Germans, between October 1 and 7.

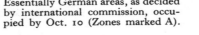 Essentially German areas, as decided by international commission, occupied by Oct. 10 (Zones marked A).

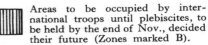 Areas to be occupied by international troops until plebiscites, to be held by the end of Nov., decided their future (Zones marked B).

1938

HOME AGAIN

Neville Chamberlain, summoned by the King, went to Buckingham Palace. Mrs. Chamberlain was there, and while thousands of people outside the palace waved and cheered, the King, the Queen, with Mr. and Mrs. Chamberlain, posed for this photograph.

AT DOWNING STREET

the Prime Minister leaned out of a window (above) and said to the crowds below: "I believe it is peace in our time . . . Go home and sleep quietly in your beds."

1938

AND SO — HITLER IN . . . BENES OUT

Whilst Czech soldiers retired, German troops marched in to the Sudeten German areas on October 1. Hitler himself, in his six-wheeled car, crossed the frontier from Germany (right) on October 3, on a victory drive through Nazi Sudetenland districts (below). At 2 p.m. on October 5, Czechoslovakia's President, Dr. Benes, resigned ; saying : "I make no criticisms . . . History will be the judge." In Prague, the Czechs, bewildered, pained and embittered by the terms of the settlement, found themselves with a new, and pro-German government. Meantime, Germany sent her envoys to Balkan countries on missions of economic penetration. And in Britain, men and women settled down again to enjoy their peace.

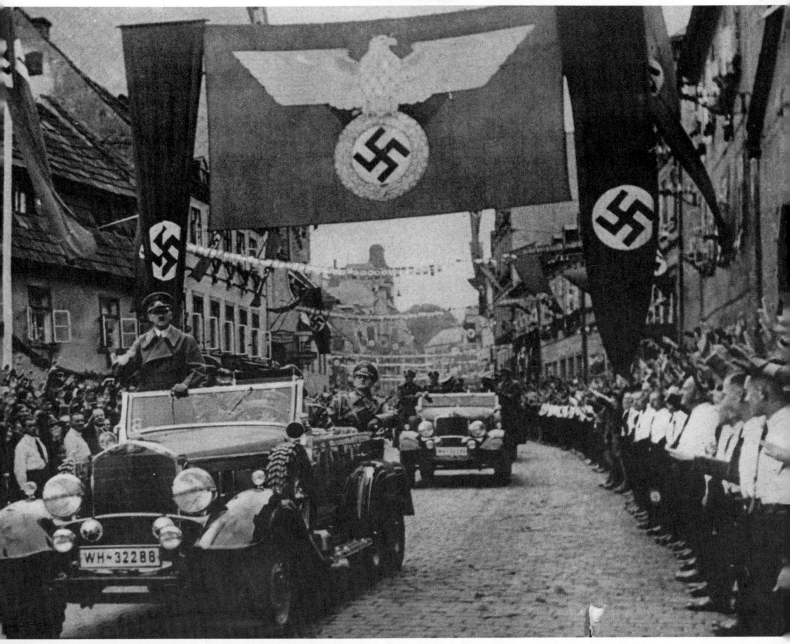

First published 1938 as *These Tremendous Years* 1919 - 1938 by The Daily Express

© The Daily Express

This edition published 1995 by
The Promotional Reprint Company Limited,
exclusively in the UK for Bookmart Limited, Desford Road,
Enderby, Leicester LE9 5AD, Coles in Canada and
Reed Editions in Australia.

ISBN 1 85648 237 5

Printed and bound in China